Accessing Your Download

The purchase of this book entitles its owner to a free download of the *Elegant Essay* e-resources: *Developing the Essayist* audio download, TEE Essay Planning Sheets, and TEE Third Edition Calendar.

To download your supplemental resources, please follow the directions below:

1. Go to our website, IEW.com
2. Sign in to your online customer account. If you do not have an account, you will need to create one.
3. After you are logged in, go to this web page: IEW.com/TEE-E
4. Click on the red download arrow.
5. You will be taken to your File Downloads page. Click on the file name, and the e-book will download onto your computer.

Please note: You are free to download and print this e-book resource as many times as needed for use within *your immediate family or classroom*. However, this information is proprietary, and we are trusting you to be on your honor not to share it with anyone. Thank you.

If you have any difficulty receiving this download after going through the steps above, please call 800.856.5815.

Institute for Excellence in Writing
8799 N. 387 Road
Locust Grove, OK 74352

The
Elegant
Essay

Student Book

Lesha Myers, M.Ed.

Third Edition, March 2011 Institute for Excellence in Writing, L.L.C.

Also by Lesha Myers:
The Elegant Essay: Building Blocks for Analytical Writing (Teacher's Manual)
Windows to the World: An Introduction to Literary Analysis
Writing Research Papers: The Essential Tools

Copyright Policy
The Elegant Essay
Building Blocks for Analytical Writing
Copyright © 2006 Lesha Myers
Third Edition, 2011
Third Printing version 2, April 2013

ISBN 978-0-9779860-1-9

Institute for Excellence in Writing
8799 N. 387 Road
Locust Grove, OK 74352
800.856.5815
info@iew.com
IEW.com

Printed in the United States of America

Table of Contents

Thank you!

I am extremely indebted to Jill Pike, Pamela White, and Maria Gerber for providing such excellent feedback, editing, and ideas for this revision. Their comments have been invaluable, especially their attention to detail.

Please visit our websites:
Lesha Myers
Cameron-Publishing.com
Click on *The Elegant Essay.*

Institute for Excellence in Writing
excellenceinwriting.com

Foreword

In 2008, I was graced with the privilege of meeting Lesha Myers at the Writing Educator's Symposium in Murrieta, California. Attending her "Arts of Arguing" session, I marveled at her passion for teaching and her desire to help students and teachers excel in their writing efforts. Her superb courses, *The Elegant Essay* and *Windows to the World: An Introduction to Literary Analysis,* were blessings to my family and became proven resources for many families working on advanced writing instruction.

My students and I enjoyed getting to know Lesha through her fine work. In her warm, friendly writing style, Lesha reveals much of herself as she gently guides her reader through the processes necessary to craft words in essays and intelligently explore and write on literature. Additionally, the teaching tools she suggested have helped me become a better teacher across the curriculum.

In 2011, I was privileged to serve as Lesha's project manager for *Writing Research Papers: The Essential Tools.* As the book was coming close to publication, Lesha confided that she was battling against cancer. Facing the storm with exceptional courage, she desired to die well so as to glorify her Lord and Savior. She did. Instead of letting the disease dictate her days, she continued teaching until the end of the school year, expressing a strong and genuine faith to the many communities she served. Lesha passed from this life on June 29, 2012.

I am grateful for all that Lesha Myers has provided for teachers and young writers. I pray that you too will enjoy getting to know her as you study her materials. Throughout her books, Lesha often invites students to contact her and share what they are learning. Please do! To continue her legacy we have assembled a team of like-minded teachers to respond to your comments and questions. You may reach them using Lesha's email address: Lesha@excellenceinwriting.com.

Blessings,
Jill Pike
Accomplished Instructor with
The Institute for Excellence in Writing

1 | OVERVIEW

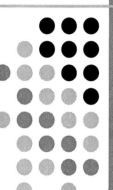

Principles

I'm a writer and I love to write. Whenever possible, I spend my free time typing on my computer or researching. Writing is one of my favorite activities.

You probably aren't like me.

You might find writing difficult.

In fact, you might actually *hate* writing.

If so, you're not alone.

Why do people find writing so distasteful? When I ask students this question, sometimes they will tell me, "It's not my gift. I don't have any talent." Other times I hear, "It's too hard" or "It takes too much time" or my all-time favorite, "When I write, I have to think."

In truth, God equips some people to excel at writing just as He gives others special talent in sports, music, academics, or other areas. On the other hand, anyone can learn the basics of writing. Anyone can learn its fundamental principles. That includes you.

Fundamental principles? Are you surprised to learn a set of *rules* undergirds all of writing? Do you suppose if you learned these rules, you might find writing easier or even (dare I say it) enjoyable?

This is exactly my hope and the reason I put this course together. I would like to introduce you to the basics of essay construction. I would like to teach you a structure to use with the essays you write. I would like to help you write an elegant essay.

Five Writing Components

Just what is this essay structure or format that I want to introduce? Follow an analogy to understand this concept. Think of the essay (or any type of writing, for that matter) as a human body. All humans share certain characteristics, yet all retain the unique stamp of the Creator. In the same way, all essays share similarities, yet each remains distinct.

Form or Structure

Essays (and all writing) embrace five different areas. The first, *form*, is like the skeletons that support people. Most skeletons look the same. They may be young or old, short or tall, male or female, but they all contain a cranium, vertebrae, femurs, and tibias. Essay form is the essay's skeleton, organization, or structure. Just as bone structure holds a person together, essays contain features that support a writer's ideas. More about this in a minute.

Content

However, beyond skeletons, people's bodies contain circulatory, respiratory, and muscular systems. They are overlaid with a wonderful covering called skin. They encompass unique personalities. You know large people and small people, healthy people and sick people, shy people and outgoing people, blondes and brunettes, and dark and light. In the same way, essays contain different *content*. You can read an essay about building a model airplane or arguing against increased taxes or comparing life in America to life in India. Content is the second part of all writing.

Style

People don't walk around *au natural*. Instead they clothe themselves with various fashions—colorful dresses or drab business suits, golf shirts or tuxedos, police uniforms or blue jeans. In the same way, authors dress essays with *style*. They might employ vivid verbs, similes, a variety of sentence openers, or many other choices. Style brings essays to life.

Mechanics

Have you ever seen a sick person, perhaps someone suffering from a lingering disease? If so, you probably saw the effects of his illness right away. He didn't look healthy. Just as people need to eat right, exercise, and treat their bodies with care, writers need to employ proper *mechanics,* such as correct grammar, punctuation, and spelling. Without these conventions, essays don't look right—they're hard to understand and follow. *Mechanics*, as the fourth part of writing, comprise the rules that govern essay health.

Voice

People have skeletons to keep them erect and hold them together, bodies and personalities to make them unique, and clothing to provide style. They operate according to a fixed set of principles to stay healthy. However, humans aren't skeletons, circulatory systems, dresses, or nutrition machines. Instead, they are people. In the same way, essays aren't form, content, style, or mechanics; rather, they are the combination of all these elements. They are essays. The way each of these separate parts combines creates their *voice*, overall effect, or personality. This final part of essay writing, *voice*, separates the good essay from the truly great.

What Is a Skeleton?

This introductory course concentrates on an essay's skeleton or structure, what holds it together, and on its content, the information it contains. We won't be as concerned with style, mechanics, and voice. Although important, you can look forward to addressing these elements in another course.

So we need to ask ourselves: "What is an essay, and what are its bones?"

The dictionary defines an essay as "a short literary composition on a particular subject," but you already knew that, didn't you? Perhaps we should ask ourselves, "What is the difference between an essay and a report?"

The difference concerns intent. A report presents basic information (such as meeting minutes or a newspaper account), while an essay provides interpretation (why the company's vice president quit or how car safety has improved). While a report provides "raw" facts, an essay provides interpretation of those facts.

(An aside: In reality facts are never "raw." Writers employ many techniques to slant a seemingly factual account of an event. One is *connotation*. Denotation is the dictionary definition of the word. I remember this because both words begin with the letter "d." Connotation, on the other hand, is its emotional impact. I could say that my dog, Tora, isn't very bright or I could say she is stupid. Although the denotation of these two phrases is similar, the connotation of one is mild and even cute, while the other is downright insulting. All facts will be interpreted according to an author's *bias*. You might look for articles in your local newspaper to see how writers employ this device. Sorry, I couldn't pass up commenting on the concept of bias. OK, now back to our regularly scheduled program.)

So, the main difference between a report and an essay is the theme, point, agenda, message, purpose, or reason for writing it in the first place. One will present information, facts, and data. The other will add personal opinion, interpretation, and commentary.

Taking a Journey

As you might imagine, especially since this course will take a number of weeks to complete, essay form or structure contains several elements. We will look at each one in turn, but first I'd like to give you an overview. To do this, I need a new analogy, so let's compare essay form to taking a journey. Your mission will be to convince me to take a trip with you.

Thesis Statement
When you plan a trip, you first decide on a destination. Where do you want to go? Why? What do you hope to accomplish on your trip? Will you rest in Hawaii to revive your tired body? Visit the monuments and governmental institutions of Washington, D.C. on a civics field trip? Increase your faith in and knowledge of the Bible by traveling to Israel and walking in the footsteps of Jesus? What is the purpose of your trip?

In the same way, you need to ask yourself why you are writing your essay. (I mean, other than the fact that your teacher requires it!) What will you write about and how will you write? Do you want to inform, describe, or persuade? What is your point and reason for writing, or as I ask my students, what are you selling? The first element of essay form is the *thesis statement*. That's a one-sentence synopsis of your entire essay and usually appears in your introduction. In the same way that you might describe your destination, "Let's go whale watching in Monterey Bay," your thesis statement describes where you want to take your reader (to Monterey Bay) and why (to go whale watching).

Introduction
Next, you will need to spend some time making your trip look inviting. Frankly, whale watching doesn't sound very exciting to me. In fact, I really don't like boats at all, especially those that sail through water. I don't want to go on your trip, so you will need to introduce your idea and convince me that it will be fun. You might begin with a funny story to melt

down my natural reluctance, or you might list some benefits I would gain by taking the trip.

The *introduction* of an essay functions in the same way. It convinces the reader to take the trip or to read on. In some ways it's the most important part of the essay, so we will spend a fair amount of time on it.

Transitions

OK, I'll go whale watching with you. I'll begin the trip, but you have the responsibility to get me to your destination. I'm not familiar with the roads in the Monterey Bay area, and I don't know my way to the wharf. You will need to bring me along and make sure I get there.

You have the same responsibility when you write essays. You need to move your reader from sentence to sentence, thought to thought, and paragraph to paragraph in a smooth way. If your reader gets lost following your logic, if he says to himself, "Huh?" he will leave you and go back home. *Transitions* keep your essay on track. They give your reader instructions such as, "I'm building on my previous thought" or "Now I'm beginning a new thought." Transitions act as road markers, giving directions and pointing the way.

Conclusions

The best part of a journey is often its completion, the return home (especially from whale watching trips). After our trip (notice I didn't talk about that part, the content), you can't leave me out in the middle of Monterey Bay; you have to bring me back to shore then back to my home. Additionally, you have to convince me the trip was worthwhile. Maybe I'll have a funny story to tell my grandchildren. Maybe I've received a benefit such as learning to cope with seasickness. Maybe you want to move me to action so I will tell others how much fun it is to bob around in a small container of wood surrounded by waves the size of houses. Perhaps I could inspire others by sharing the wonder of encountering one of the largest of God's majestic sea creatures (and, in truth, the experience *was* truly awesome).

In the same way, you need a *conclusion* to your essay, a way to bring your reader back to the place he started, but with something added. Perhaps you've added knowledge by telling him about your favorite American hero or moved him to reconsider his position on a controversial issue or brightened his day by sharing a humorous story. The last part of your essay, the conclusion, ties all of your thoughts together.

Now that we've discussed an overview of where we are going in this course, let's get started. It's time to begin our journey.

Notes

Use this page to take notes as your teacher directs.

Five Writing Components

1. Form — *structure — Basic Bones of essay intre, thesis, transition, Body, conclusion*

2. Content — *topic — information and opinion*

3. Style — *sentence openers, vivid verbs, descriptive, dress ups Bring essay to Life*

4. Mechanics

5. Voice

Bias

Essay Parts

➢ Thesis Statement

➢ Introduction

➢ (Body)

➢ Transitions

➢ Conclusion

2 | THESIS STATEMENTS

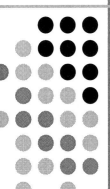

What Is a Thesis Statement?

If you have written a paragraph, you are probably familiar with the concept of a topic sentence, usually the first sentence in your paragraph that introduces your topic or main idea. A thesis statement is similar to a topic sentence. A topic sentence usually begins a paragraph and tells readers what to expect from it, and a thesis statement does the same for an entire essay. You can think of a thesis statement as a mega-topic sentence. Often, it can act as a one-sentence summary of your essay. It's your essay's mission statement.

English handbooks usually define a thesis statement as

- **a statement of purpose, intent, or main idea of an essay**

Think of the thesis statement as a compass. Like a compass, it gives direction and points the way:

➢ **For your readers,** the thesis statement keeps their brains on track, moving their thoughts towards your point. It establishes boundaries. If an essay traveled outside the bounds of its thesis statement, your reader might become confused. Confused readers stop reading.

➢ **For you as the writer,** the thesis statement also helps keep the essay on track. Writing choices abound. Should you include this fact, that detail, or another story? A well-formulated thesis statement outlining your essay's purpose will help you decide what to include and what to leave out. For research papers, it can also help you manage your time. You might decide to skim a book or website rather than read it thoroughly if it falls on the outskirts of your thesis.

Kinds of Thesis Statements

Expository, Narrative, & Persuasive

Most essays contain a thesis statement to give form and scope and state the author's point—why he or she took the time to write the essay in the first place. In an *expository* essay, which explains or informs, the thesis statement will narrow the focus of the explanation, such as how to choose a family pet, or the information, such as methods used to design and construct Hoover Dam. In a *narrative* essay, which is a story with a purpose, the thesis statement will reveal a lesson that the author learned or an emotion that he wants to share or relive. In a *persuasive* essay, which tries to change the reader's mind, the thesis statement will present the claim or argument the author wants to convince you to adopt. In an essay, the thesis statement glues thoughts together.

Working Thesis Statements

Let's say you have settled on a topic for your essay and you write a thesis statement. However, it has issues. It's dull, boring, and lifeless. No problem. Just call it a *working thesis statement* and you'll be fine. A working thesis statement is a preliminary statement of purpose that can keep your thoughts organized and your essay on track. If you change directions, just change your thesis. At the end of your writing, revisit it and see if you can breathe some life into it as you polish it up.

Occasionally, my students tell me they don't want to feel confined by a thesis statement. Rather, they want to begin their essay and see where it leads. This idea has some merit. Sometimes my writing takes on a life of its own, and what I end up with bears no resemblance to what I originally intended to convey. On the other hand, writing is thinking. You must use your brain at some point. You can use it before you begin writing, during your writing, or after you are finished during the editing step. If you wait until your rough draft is complete to develop a thesis statement, you might find it hard to locate a controlling or unifying idea, and you might have to discard some of your work. Giving thought to your thesis before you begin to write might actually save you time.

Academic Thesis Statements

If you write for people in the academic world, especially history or science teachers, you might need to write a three-pronged thesis statement to introduce the three main points of your paper. This gives focus for a busy teacher who may have a stack of papers to read. Additionally, an *academic thesis* makes a great working thesis because it clarifies your thoughts and forces you to constantly ask yourself whether or not you should include a particular detail in your essay. The academic thesis statement does the following:

- announces the essay's topics or arguments.
- usually occurs at the end of the introductory paragraph.
- completes the unspoken statement, "In this essay, I will [inform, describe, argue, or defend] this topic in these three ways."
- echoes the topics of the three main body paragraphs.

A thesis statement is like a big beach umbrella covering your essay and helping you to make choices about what information to include and what to pass by. Ask yourself, "Does this topic add something to my essay? Does it fit under the umbrella of my thesis statement?" If so, include it. If not, leave it, or change your thesis statement.

Developing Thesis Statements

In my experience, developing a thesis statement is one of the highest hurdles students need to hop over to write elegant essays. To help, I impose a few artificial rules on my beginning and intermediate students. First, the thesis may not be longer than one sentence. Although a thesis statement might span several sentences under the direction of an accomplished writer, beginners will focus better if they have fewer options. Second, the thesis must be the last sentence in the introduction. When students move on to more advanced essay structures, the thesis can move, too and discard these artificial rules.

The Elegant Essay

Steps to create a thesis statement

To generate a thesis statement, follow these three steps:

1. Determine your essay's intent. Will it inform, describe, or persuade?
2. Narrow your focus or your topic. Instead of writing about Scotland, you might choose a specific aspect of Scotland—famous castles or the origin of golf, for example. Make sure you can explain your topic in the time and space allotted to you. A one-page paper requires a very narrow topic, while ten pages would let you broaden it.
3. Develop a two-part statement. In part one, state your narrow focus. In part two, add details concerning what you want to say about it.

Some examples follow.

Types of Thesis Statements

	Expository or Informative Essay	Narrative or Descriptive Essay	Persuasive Essay
Definition	Gives information on a particular topic.	Describes a person, place, idea, or event. Tells a story with a purpose.	Reasons and argues to change a reader's viewpoint or perspective.
Essay Types	Most biographies, reports, directions and instructions, analysis, and other essays that offer some or little interpretation.	Travelogues, personal narratives, some biographies, nostalgia, and writing that appeals to the five senses.	Any essay that makes an assertion and calls for the reader to agree or disagree with the writer's conclusion. Some literary analysis essays.
Purpose of Thesis	• Announces the essay's subject • States the topic(s) • Completes the unspoken statement, "What I want to say is that…" or "This essay will tell you about…"	• Describes the mood or emotion the writer wishes to impart • Expresses a feeling • Completes the unspoken statement, "This essay will make you feel or experience…"	• States the position you want to defend, what you believe, or what you want to explore • Takes a stand • Completes the unspoken statement, "This essay will explore or make you believe or persuade you to…"
Thesis Example	Men and women who wish to protect their country's freedoms can choose to serve in five different branches of the military.	As the movie ended, I thought about my grandfather's sacrifice on Iwo Jima and how his courage allowed me to live in freedom.	Women have no business endangering their country's security by serving alongside men on battlefields. or If women excel in civilian jobs, they can undoubtedly make positive contributions to the military.

More Thesis Statement Examples

Intent	Topic	Focus/Slant/Details	Thesis Example
Inform	Golf	Began in Scotland	The game of golf originated in Scotland.
Inform	Paul's third journey	Spread Christianity	Paul spread Christianity to thousands on his third missionary journey.
Describe	Me on September 11th	Fear	As I watched events unfold on that fateful Tuesday, I shuddered to think perhaps they foretold the beginning of WWIII.
Describe	Contestants	Anticipation	The girls eagerly huddled around the announcer and waited for the judges' decision.
Persuade	Television	Beneficial	TV's educational programs expand a child's experience.
Persuade	Sports	Steroids	Steroid use destroys the competitive spirit of professional sports.

Working or Academic Thesis Statement Examples

Intent	Subject	Three Topics	Thesis Example
Inform	History of golf	In Scotland In England In the United States	The game of golf originated in Scotland, moved to England, but hit its swing in the United States.
Inform	Sports	Baseball Football Hockey	America's favorite sports include baseball, football, and hockey.
Describe	Hawaiian vacation	Refreshment Economy Culture	Stressed-out people journey to Hawaii to refresh their spirits, support the economy, and experience a different culture.
Persuade	Daytime curfews	Freedom Taxes Ineffective	Daytime curfews infringe on the freedom of minors, waste taxpayers' money, and prove ineffective.
Persuade	Television	Obesity Inappropriate Content Solitude	Unmonitored television viewing harms children physically, mentally, and socially.

Notes

Use this page to take notes as your teacher directs.

Purpose of a Thesis Statement (Function)

Kinds of Theses by Essay Type (Genre)

1. Narrative (descriptive)

2. Expository (Informative)

3. Persuasive (argumentative)

Working Thesis Statements

Academic Thesis Statements

Steps to Create Thesis Statements

1.

2.

3.

Thesis Modeling Notes

Essay Type	Topic	Focus/Slant/Details	Possible Thesis
Expository (Informative)	Friends	Loving the unlovable	
		Overcoming shyness	
		Bible verses	
Narrative (Descriptive)	Holidays	Nostalgic	
		Time for family	
		Stressful/hectic	
Persuasive	Television	Harmful	
		Wasteful	
		Enjoyable	
Academic/ Informative	Career	Fulfilling Secure Profitable	
Academic/ Persuasive	Smoking	Health Cost Image	

Thesis Statements

Directions: For each of the subjects below, choose an essay type, decide on a slant or details, and write a thesis statement. You must use each of the essay types (to describe, inform, or persuade) at least once and one example of a three-pronged academic thesis.

1.   Courage

       Circle essay type: describe, inform, or persuade

       Focus /Slant/Details _____

       Thesis

       _____

       _____

2.   A gift

       Circle essay type: describe, inform, or persuade

       Focus /Slant/Details _____

       Thesis

       _____

       _____

3.   Women in the military

       Circle essay type: describe, inform, or persuade

       Focus /Slant/Details _____opertonfiy_____

       Thesis _there is opertojntr ForeDvcation For woman _____

       _in the military_____

4.   Education

       Circle essay type: describe, inform, or persuade

       Focus /Slant/Details _____

       Thesis

       _____

       _____

Thesis Statements

Directions: For each of the subjects below, choose an essay type, decide on a slant or details, and write a thesis statement. You must use each of the essay types (to describe, inform, or persuade) at least once and one example of a three-pronged academic thesis.

1.   Socialism

      Circle essay type: describe, inform, or persuade

      Focus/Slant/Details _____

      Thesis

      _____

      _____

2.   A favorite teacher

      Circle essay type: describe, inform, or persuade

      Focus/Slant/Details _____

      Thesis

      _____

      _____

3.   College

      Circle essay type: describe, inform, or persuade

      Focus/Slant/Details _____

      Thesis

      _____

      _____

4.   Ministry or community service

      Circle essay type: describe, inform, or persuade

      Focus/Slant/Details _____

      Thesis

      _____

      _____

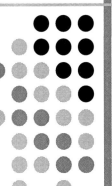

3 | ESSAY ORGANIZATION

The Body

OK, you have your topic. You know what you are going to write about, at least in theory, and you've developed a thesis statement. You may not like your thesis statement, but it works and will get you started. What's next?

Logic and sequence say the introduction. However, I have had more success teaching my students to write from the inside out—that is, at least for the first several times, to write the essay's body before its introduction. To do this, you will need to understand *organization*.

Organization entails the way you put your essay together and how you arrange its content. That's the subject of this section.

The Five-Paragraph Organization

Most beginning essays span five paragraphs (introduction, three body paragraphs, and a conclusion). You can develop a good essay—not too long or not too short—in three body paragraphs, but there is nothing sacred about the number three. You could write a four-paragraph, or a six-paragraph, or a twenty-paragraph essay and employ the same techniques.

I'm going to offer you several ways to structure your essays, beginning with a very simple structure and moving on to some that are more complex. The simple structure will help you if you are just beginning to write essays, but the concept will also help more experienced students write a short essay or write under a time constraint. If you have to write an essay in thirty-minutes to pass some sort of test, the simple structure will serve you well, although you may not have enough time to complete five paragraphs.

The Simplest Structure

Your first challenge will be to select a topic to address in each body paragraph and write a working thesis. If you've written an academic thesis, its three prongs will be the topics of your three body paragraphs. Perhaps you are writing an essay on courage, and your thesis statement reads as follows:

➢ People display courage every day when they stand firm in their beliefs, do something hard, or hold their sinful nature in check.

You could begin your introduction by relating an amazing story of courage—a young man rescuing his neighbor from a burning home, for example—then move on to ordinary everyday kinds of courage, and conclude with your thesis statement. Your next three paragraphs could discuss courage as it relates to upholding personal convictions, completing a difficult task, and not responding rashly.

The Simple Structure

A good way to organize your body paragraphs is to employ the acronym SEE, which stands for Statement, Explanation, or Example. Begin with a topic sentence, follow it with two SEEs, and end with a clincher. Whenever you feel at a loss for words, you can use this form for inspiration. But remember, this is just to get you started. As you become more comfortable with writing, you will want to exercise your own creativity and move beyond the formula.

I. Topic Sentence

Begin with your topic sentence. It should tie in to your thesis statement (in this case firm convictions) and explain how you will address the topic in your paragraph. In our example you might say, "Ordinary people display courage when they stand firm in their personal convictions."

A. First Statement (S)

Next, make an assertion or statement about your topic sentence. An assertion is a declaration or something you want to prove or discuss. In our example we might say, "Peer pressure sometimes prevents people from listening to their consciences."

1. First Statement Explanation (E) or Example (E)

Follow your assertion or statement with two sentences of explanation. You might develop the statement by expanding on it or explaining it in more detail, offering a story, giving an example, or in the case that follows, making an observation. In discussing courage and peer pressure you might say, "A young person might hear companions spreading false rumors or gossiping about a close friend. Speaking out, even graciously, takes fortitude."

B. Second Statement (S)

After you've developed your first assertion as much as you like (two sentences at a minimum), follow it with another statement that relates to your topic. Pay attention to your transition to make sure this statement connects with your first. You could say, "Alternatively, people might face the temptation to set aside their standards."

1. Second Statement Explanation (E) or Example (E)

Just as you did for your first assertion, follow with at least two more sentences of evidence, details, or examples. In our example, "If friends want to watch a movie filled with violence or inappropriate content, the person faces a quandary. Should he go along with the group and watch or affirm his standards and leave?"

II. Clincher Statement

Finally, conclude your paragraph with a final or closing statement that reflects the topic sentence. For example, "By exhibiting courage, people stay true to their beliefs and principles."

The simple structure is a good place to start because it contains all of the elements of a well-structured paragraph: topic and clincher sentences, transitions, and on-topic discussion. It is the simplest; it is not always the best. Use it when you're under time pressure, when you are experiencing brain freeze, or for a first draft—or even a pre-draft when you just want to get words down on the paper. For better and more elegant essays, you need more. Read on.

Showing vs. Telling

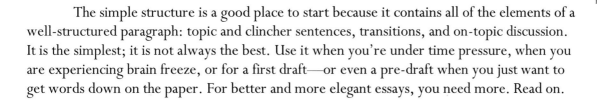

Most English books tell you that you need evidence and support for your paragraph topics, and this is true, but what exactly is *support*? I find it easier to think in terms of *telling* and *showing*. Telling is exactly what it sounds like—you tell your reader what you are going to talk about. Showing, on the other hand, demonstrates and expands your point. It creates a picture or impression in your reader's brain. What is the problem with the simple structure demonstrated above? It is almost all telling. It needs some showing. Here are some examples of the difference between telling and showing.

Telling	*Showing*
The Internet makes shopping convenient. (informative)	I wanted to buy a conch shell to use as a prop when I taught *Lord of the Flies*. I could have searched local shops, probably in vain, or made long distant phone calls to other parts of the country. Instead, I fired up Google, typed in "conch shell sales," and ten minutes later a business in Florida wrapped, shipped, and prepared to deliver the shell right to my mailbox.
My dog was scared. (descriptive)	Tora's tail uncurled and her ears drooped. She backed up behind the table leg, bared her teeth, and growled softly.
Smoking destroys your health. (persuasive)	If you are a teenager and you continue to smoke for the rest of your life, you have a fifty-fifty chance of dying from tobacco-related diseases. Even if you beat the odds, you still have a 25 percent chance of sacrificing 21 years of your life.

By all means, you need to *tell* in your essay, but you also need to *show*. To say this another way, you need to make statements and assertions, but you also need to back them up with support or evidence. Your primary asserting, your *telling* occurs in your thesis. The rest of your essay responds to the reader's unspoken question (Read with your best British accent.), "I say, Old Man, you'll have to convince me." That takes showing.

Evidence and Support—Showing
So what can you use for support in your essay? Plenty. Let's look at some ideas.

Evidence Examples

Besides developing a thesis statement, the skill my students find most difficult when learning to write elegant essays is providing evidence and support for their points. Therefore, I thought I would provide a few examples of what students might generate and how they could improve their body paragraphs.

Example One

Many people in today's society depend on the Internet's information. A lot of people read the news off Internet sites such as CNN.com. The Internet is more efficient because there are many newspapers that do not cover everything that happens. On the Internet people can search many sites for a variety of news—current or archived. People might find different types of information on the Internet, including facts, opinions, how-tos, and even information on people. The Internet bursts with information.

This paragraph is well-structured. It includes a topic sentence that relates to the thesis statement, several body sentences, and a clincher to wrap it up. It's grammatically correct and thoughtful. However, it is almost all telling and somewhat redundant. The student is telling me about the Internet's information; he is not showing me how to obtain that information. He has no evidence to back up his claims. Here are some ideas (in italics) for additions:

Today, people depend on the Internet for information. A lot of people get their news directly from Internet sites, such as CNN.com. This offers advantages over newspapers because newspapers do not include all of the news and are not always current. *A while back I wanted to know the results of the special election in my district, and I did not have access to a newspaper. I powered up my Internet, typed "Concord California local election results" into a search engine, and within seconds the results appeared on my screen.* The Internet contains other types of information as well, including facts, opinions, and even information about people. *If you type a person's phone number into Google, you will learn his full name and address, complete with a map and driving directions to his home. You can even view a satellite photo of his home.* The Internet bursts with information.

Example Two

Before we get too excited about human cloning, we need to recognize the many dangers involved in the process. Before scientists even implant the clone in the surrogate mother, there are difficulties. Those who do get their fling at living have serious health issues and defects as well. Not counting the aging problem, clones still do not have it easy. Serious health impairments result. Clones' problems include underdeveloped body organs and immune systems, diabetes, anemia, skin infections, blood vessel abnormalities, grossly enlarged placentas and umbilical cords, fatty livers, hypertension, misshapen heads, and lung disease. Would we really want to curse a human baby with these defects?

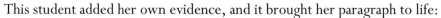

This student added her own evidence, and it brought her paragraph to life:

> Before we get too excited about human cloning, we need to recognize the many dangers involved in the process. Before scientists even implant the clone in the surrogate mother, there are difficulties. *Cloning is a difficult process with a very low success rate. Only two percent of the cloned animals are suitable for implantation. Of those two percent, 97 out of 100 do not survive. Whether human or animal, that is still an enormous figure. If those are human cloned babies, they are individual people who are dying, failing to get a chance to live like other people.* Those who do get their fling at living have serious health issues and defects as well. *For starters, they age early. Dolly was suffering from arthritis at the age of five years, whereas arthritis usually strikes sheep of advanced ages, like nine or ten.* Not counting the aging problem, clones still do not have it easy. *Many cloned animals have health issues including Dolly, Second Chance, Noah, and a little six-month old lamb with a bad problem of hyperventilating.* Clones' problems include underdeveloped body organs and immune systems, diabetes, anemia, skin infections, blood vessel abnormalities, grossly enlarged placentas and umbilical cords, fatty livers, hypertension, misshapen heads, and lung disease. Would we really want to curse a human baby with these defects?

The difference between the simple example introduced a few pages ago (SEE) and this one is the support. The more support or evidence or proof you can bring to your essay, the more you will convince your audience that you are informed and worth listening to. Instead of *telling* readers to believe something, to take you on faith, you *show* them the evidence and lead them to make up their own minds. Let's look at some ways to do this.

More Evidence & Support Examples

There are at least eight ways to show and support:

1. Examples—a specific instance
2. Personal Experience—something that has actually happened to you that sheds light on the topic
3. Statistics—numbers, percents, and data
4. Research/Testimony—a quote or summary of an authority or specialist's views
5. Observation—a judgment or inference; logical reasoning
6. Description—word pictures that bring your idea to life
7. Anecdote—a story that relates to or exemplifies the point you are trying to make
8. Analogy—a comparison to something else to clarify your reasoning

To illustrate the eight options for body evidence and support, several examples for body paragraphs follow. These same techniques could be used for *showing* in all elegant essays.

Example

An example is a specific illustration of your point that occurs outside your personal experience. It could be the experience of a friend or relative, or it could be something you hear or read about.

> One benefit television offers is immediate access to worldwide news. Broadcasts allow people to learn about events happening all around the globe. On Christmas Day in 2004, while most people were wrapped up in the events of the day or unwrapping their presents, television reports shared some unsettling news: In one of the worst natural disasters in recent history, a tsunami had roared across the shores of several Southeast Asian countries, killing thousands. In short order, news shows reported the devastation, which allowed Americans to drop to their knees in prayer and open their pocketbooks in tangible support. The images broadcast on television allowed people to see the effects of the tsunami and quickly help the sufferers of this dreadful disaster.

Personal Experience

Personal experience is similar to an example. However, examples report other people's experience, while personal experience conveys your own. If you use personal experience as support for your essay, please remember two things: First, it is perfectly fine to lapse into first person point of view and use personal pronouns (such as *I, me, my, we, our, us*) while relating your details. Second, personal experience must be true. It would be highly unethical to fabricate information and write about it as if it really happened and damage your credibility.

> It's hard to master writing body paragraphs. Not only do students have to remember a variety of techniques, they have to think. Thinking is arduous work. In my twenty-plus years of teaching composition in one form or another, I've rarely seen students who master these techniques immediately. Instead, they have to practice. Then they have to practice some more. Finally, one day it all comes together, and their writing becomes a joy to read.

Statistics

Statistics, the use of figures and numbers to make a point, can effectively support your essay's topics. However, you need to be aware of several potential difficulties. First, any statistics you use need to come from reliable sources. You will need to exercise discernment to determine whether or not you may trust the statistics. Second, statistics can be overwhelming, especially if you use too many. Readers might get lost in a sea of numbers. After you use statistics, be sure to apply them or comment on them. Tell your readers what you want them to learn from your use of the statistics.

> Television, especially unmonitored or excessive viewing, can harm children's development. Many shows, even those aired during the evening family hour, contain unnecessary and extreme violence. According to the Parents Television Council, by the time the average American child reaches his eighteenth birthday, his mind will have been polluted with 200,000 violent images. Additionally, he will have witnessed 8,000 brutal murders. This is too much. How many children have personally witnessed even one murder in real life? Very few. Parents must protect innocent young minds from television's refuse.

Please note that when you cite statistics or expert testimony, the reference needs to be cited in a Works Cited page. The citation used in the above paragraph would look like this:

"TV Bloodbath: Violence on Prime Time Broadcast TV." *Parents Television Council.* N.d. Web. 30 Jun. 2010.

Observation

Observations might also be called logical reasoning. Beginning with a premise or set of facts, you build a case for your arguments by reasoning or making inferences. Words that frequently occur with this type of evidence or support include *might* or *could*. The above paragraph illustrating the use of statistics might have ended this way if it included an observation:

> Children who watch violence might imitate it. With seared consciences, they might not be able to discern right actions from wrong actions.

Generally, observation that contains speculation, like the above example, is the weakest kind of support. Think twice before you use it.

Research or Testimony

Oftentimes it's helpful to find an expert who can lend weight to your arguments. What is an *expert?* Loosely defined, it is someone who can be trusted to speak with authority on the topic or someone with experience in the field. These days, the Internet abounds with research and expert testimony. As with statistics, you will need to exercise discernment to determine whether or not the testimony is from an authority or a dependable source.

> Scientists play god when they engage in embryonic stem cell research because they determine who has the right to live and who will die. Just because an embryo has not developed to the point of birth does not mean it is not a human being. According to Dr. Francis J. Beckwith, fellow of The Center for Bioethics and Human Dignity, "The unborn—from zygote to blastocyst to embryo to fetus—is the same being, the same substance, that develops into an adult." If it is wrong to kill an adult, it is equally wrong to kill an embryo, even if the embryo's stem cells might save another's life.

Beckwith, Francis J. PhD. "What Would Reagan Do?" *National Review Online.* 27 July 2004. 20 Feb. 2006. <http://www.nationalreview.com/comment/beckwith200407270012.asp>.

Description

Unlike the written word, photographs and movies portray vivid images that make an impact. Writing, especially descriptive writing, strives to create an image in the reader's mind that makes the same impact. Good descriptions contain imagery and appeal to the five senses.

> Smoking causes lung cancer and a host of other life-shortening diseases. Years of inhaling tar and nicotine produce cancerous lungs: black, shriveled, and stunted. They look like burned cookies left in the oven so long their edges crisp and curl until they resemble charcoal lumps. It's no wonder victims of lung cancer lose weight and cough up blood.

Anecdote / Story

Stories and anecdotes bring essays to life; however, they must be true stories. As with personal experience, it is highly unethical to invent details and pass them off as true.

> Bev Holzrichter owes her life to the Internet. During foaling season in 2005, Ms. Holzrichter entered her horse barn and felt the wrath of a mare trying to protect her colt. Thankfully, friends from around the world watched the accident on webcams installed to allow the global community to share the miracle of foaling season. The Charlotte, Iowa, Rescue Squad received calls from Germany, the United Kingdom, and France, and help arrived quickly. Not only does the Internet foster communication, it can make the difference between life and death.

Analogy

An analogy is a way to compare two dissimilar items or ideas. By linking something known to something less familiar, an analogy creates a likeness and consequently, understanding. One of my students thought of the following brilliant analogy:

> Salary caps allow fair competition in sports because they limit the aggregate amount of money any one team can spend on its players' salaries. This prevents any team with an abundance of funds from hiring all superstars. Salary caps are like trips to the gas station: A person pays the attendant $40 and proceeds to pump his gas. When he reaches his limit, the pump shuts down. In the same way, when a team reaches its salary cap, it can't spend any more money on players. Owners must budget their payroll carefully, which creates a leveling effect and promotes fair competition in the league.

All of the examples above can be profitably used for narrative or descriptive, informative or expository, and persuasive essays. Additionally, they may be combined, often in the same paragraph. But don't lose sight of your point. Remember, the purpose of evidence and support is to uphold and prove your thesis statement. Argue your premise, describe your event, or explain your process. Use these techniques for *showing*: for emphasis, proof, and backup.

Notes

Use this page to take notes as your teacher directs.

The Simple Structure

1. Format (Topic + SEE + Clincher)

2. Limitations (and when to use)

Modeling

Example #1

Peer pressure sometimes prevents people from listening to their consciences. A young person might hear companions spreading false rumors or gossiping about a close friend. No one wants to go against the crowd. Speaking out, even graciously, takes fortitude. Alternatively, people might face the temptation to set aside their standards. If friends want to watch a movie filled with violence or inappropriate content, the person faces a quandary. Should he go along with the group and watch or affirm his standards and leave? By exhibiting courage, people stay true to their beliefs and principles.

Example #2

When parents give gifts to their children, they send a special message of love. They say they care in a very real way. For example, if a child wants a computer for Christmas, parents might work hard to provide it. They might even sacrifice receiving their own gifts to buy it. Their actions communicate their love.

Example #3

When parents give gifts to their children, they send a special message of love. They say that they care in a very real way.

_____

_____

_____

_____

_____

_____

_____

_____

_____

_____

_____

_____

_____

_____

_____

_____

Their actions communicated their love.

Showing vs. Telling

Telling	Showing
Dad is very funny.	
Mom sometimes forgets things.	
The cat was afraid of Tora, the very brave dog.	
[Your favorite sport] is fun.	

Evidence & Support for Essays

1. Examples

2. Personal Experience

3. Statistics

4. Research/Testimony

5. Observation

6. Description

7. Anecdote

8. Analogy

Body Paragraphs

Refer to the thesis statements you generated in a previous lesson. Select two thesis statements, revise them if you wish, and write one body paragraph for each, practicing the options for evidence and support—for showing—described in this lesson.

Topics: courage, a gift, women in the military, education

1. Circle essay type: describe, inform, or persuade

   Support options: example, personal experience, statistics, expert testimony, observation, description, anecdote or story, or analogy

   Thesis:
   _____
   _____

   Body:
   _____
   _____
   _____
   _____
   _____
   _____
   _____

2. Circle essay type: describe, inform, or persuade

   Support options: example, personal experience, statistics, expert testimony, observation, description, anecdote or story, or analogy

   Thesis:
   _____
   _____

   Body:
   _____
   _____
   _____
   _____
   _____

Body Paragraphs

Refer to the thesis statements you generated in a previous lesson. Select two thesis statements, revise them if you wish, and write one body paragraph for each, practicing the options for evidence and support—for showing—described in this lesson.

Topics: courage, a gift, women in the military, education

1. Circle essay type: describe, inform, or persuade

    Support options: example, personal experience, statistics, expert testimony, observation, description, anecdote or story, or analogy

    Thesis:

    _____

    _____

    Body:

    _____

    _____

    _____

    _____

    _____

    _____

2. Circle essay type: describe, inform, or persuade

    Support options: example, personal experience, statistics, expert testimony, observation, description, anecdote or story, or analogy

    Thesis:

    _____

    _____

    Body:

    _____

    _____

    _____

    _____

    _____

The Elegant Essay

Body Paragraphs

Refer to the thesis statements you generated in a previous lesson. Select two thesis statements, revise them if you wish, and write one body paragraph for each, practicing the options for evidence and support—for showing—*described in this lesson.*

Topics: socialism, a favorite teacher, college, ministry or community service

1. Circle essay type: describe, inform, or persuade

   Support options: example, personal experience, statistics, expert testimony, observation, description, anecdote or story, or analogy

   Thesis:

   _____

   _____

   Body:

   _____

   _____

   _____

   _____

   _____

   _____

   _____

2. Circle essay type: describe, inform, or persuade

   Support options: example, personal experience, statistics, expert testimony, observation, description, anecdote or story, or analogy

   Thesis:

   _____

   _____

   Body:

   _____

   _____

   _____

   _____

   _____

   _____

Body Paragraphs

Refer to the thesis statements you generated in a previous lesson. Select two thesis statements, revise them if you wish, and write one body paragraph for each, practicing the options for evidence and support—for showing—described in this lesson.

Topics: socialism, a favorite teacher, college, ministry or community service

1. Circle essay type: describe, inform, or persuade

   Support options: example, personal experience, statistics, expert testimony, observation, description, anecdote or story, or analogy

   Thesis:

   _____

   _____

   Body:

   _____

   _____

   _____

   _____

   _____

   _____

2. Circle essay type: describe, inform, or persuade

   Support options: example, personal experience, statistics, expert testimony, observation, description, anecdote or story, or analogy

   Thesis:

   _____

   _____

   Body:

   _____

   _____

   _____

   _____

   _____

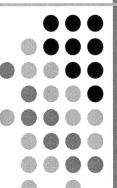

4 TRANSITIONS

Road Signs

Have you ever found yourself totally lost while reading an article? Somehow and some-where, you lost the thread of the author's thoughts. You backtrack and notice he moved to a different subject without informing you. You missed his transition.

Transitions move readers' thoughts along the writer's track. They connect or relate one idea or thought to another. Connecting each point smoothly, transitions indicate changes in time (sequence), in place (space), or in mood (atmosphere). English handbooks define transitions as words or phrases that help tie ideas together. In the same way that traffic signs guide cars, transitions guide thought. They help the reader keep up with the writer.

Kinds of Transitions

The Yellow Line
(called* reference transitions *in English handbooks)
The first type of transition connects thoughts from sentence to sentence within a paragraph. It functions similarly to the yellow line on a road, which keeps cars moving along in their proper lane. A smooth paragraph with good flow usually contains good transitions. Jumpy paragraphs with potholes, or unconnected thoughts, lack them. Yellow line transitions include

> ➤ pronouns which refer back to their antecedents, or the pronoun that replaces the noun.
> ➤ repeated words from the previous sentence.
> ➤ synonyms of a word used in a previous sentence.
> ➤ restated thoughts from previous sentences.

Road Signs
(called* connectives *in English handbooks)
The second type of transition signals a change in thought in the same way a road sign signals a change in direction (stop, curve ahead, yield, or even soft shoulder). Road sign transitions might include

> ➤ continuing after a stop sign: likewise, in addition, mostly, more important, thus, in other words, first, then, next.
> ➤ changing direction: on the other hand, but, however, nevertheless.
> ➤ detouring down a side road: for instance, such as, for example, like.
> ➤ reaching the destination: finally, and so, to sum up.

Bridges

The final type of transition links thoughts between paragraphs. Acting as a bridge, these transitions move the reader from one thought, idea, or topic to another. Bridge transitions use a combination of yellow line and road sign techniques to hook paragraphs together. The topic sentence of one paragraph often repeats words or thoughts from the clincher or last statement of the previous paragraph. Additionally, it contains transitional words as needed.

Bridge Example

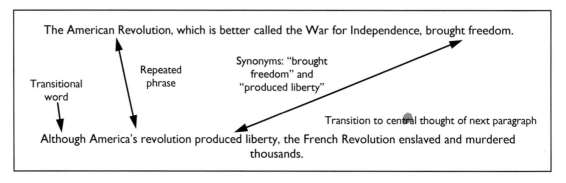

Problems With Transitions

Besides omitting them, the biggest problem students encounter with transitions is word over-use. Readers will tire if you use the same word excessively. Get out your *Synonym Finder* or thesaurus and see if you can find appropriate substitutes. Some suggestions follow:

1. ADDITION:
   and, third, similarly, also, likewise, furthermore, too, and then, in addition, in fact, next, further, at the same time, again, finally, by the same token, first, besides, equally important, second, moreover, more than this

2. CONTRAST:
   but, contrarily, notwithstanding, yet, after all, on the contrary, still, on the other hand, however, nevertheless, at the same time

3. RESULT:
   hence, therefore, it follows that, thus, consequently, since this is true, then, accordingly, under these circumstances

4. ALTERNATION:
   or, as, so not, but also, nor both, and the one, else, either, or the other, otherwise, neither, nor, on the one hand, while, on the other hand

5. CAUSE:
   for, because, now that, as, inasmuch as, owing to, since, seeing that

6. REPETITION, EXEMPLIFICATION, INTENSIFICATION:
   in fact, in short, in other words, indeed, in brief, that is to say, for instance, that is, for example, namely, thus, to be sure

7. PURPOSE:
   that, so that, for this purpose, lest, in order that

Notes

Use this page to take notes as your teacher directs.

Purpose of Transitions

Kinds of Transitions

1. Yellow Line (reference transitions)
   Pronouns: Last Saturday afternoon, Tom went to the movies. He saw a terrific show.
   Repeated words: As to special effects, they were incredible, and Tom immediately came home to research how they were done.
   Synonyms: Surprisingly, his investigation revealed that the movie studio had found a way to create a new interface between computer generated graphics and film.
   Repeated thoughts: Learning about how the special effects were created made Tom appreciate the movie even more.

2. Road Signs (connectors)

3. Bridges (paragraph hooks)

Modeling

1. One thousand students have taken advantage of this opportunity since it began in 1985.
2. "I've heard a lot of great feedback from the program. So many students are really glad they went," commented Dr. Thomas Johnson, the study's organizer.
3. For more information contact the university at 999-9999 or www.university.com.
4. Students can participate in other international study programs, including Brazil, Mexico, and Spain.
5. The London staff focuses on art, history, and humanities.
6. The course is challenging.
7. Students at the local university can earn the opportunity to study in London or Paris.
8. Time for field trips is included.

_____

_____

_____

_____

_____

_____

Potential Problems with Transitions

Directions: Put the following sentences in order; then add transitional words or phrases between sentences to form a complete paragraph. Do not change the substance of any thoughts although you may combine sentences and change the wording.

1. There will be two kite competition groups: twelve and over, and under twelve.
2. Participants may bring a picnic.
3. The public is invited to fly a kite or watch demonstrations.
4. The event is free.
5. Last year's event drew 300 participants.
6. Cool Kite Competition was organized to attract the public to the newly refurbished reservoirs.
7. Winners will receive gift certificates to Cool Kites.
8. Kites will soar over our town in the second annual Cool Kite Competition next month.

_____

_____

_____

_____

_____

_____

_____

_____

_____

_____

_____

_____

_____

_____

_____

_____

_____

_____

_____

_____

_____

Directions: Put the following sentences in order; then add transitional words or phrases between sentences to form a complete paragraph. Do not change the substance of any thoughts although you may combine sentences and change the wording.

1. We will grow like Him.
2. The soldier fights for his captain and shares in his captain's victory.
3. The believer contends for Christ and partakes of his Master's triumph.
4. "For me to live is Christ" (Philippians 1:21).
5. Christ is the object of our life.
6. We live in near fellowship with the Lord Jesus.
7. We seek to tread in His footsteps.

_____

_____

_____

_____

_____

_____

_____

_____

_____

_____

_____

_____

_____

_____

_____

_____

_____

_____

_____

_____

_____

_____

Notes

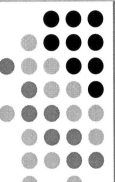

5 | INTRODUCTIONS

Openings

How do you decide whether or not to read an article? Do you read the first few sentences just to see if it's interesting? And if it's not, do you ever put it down? I know I do. There are so many words and so little time. I need to be selective. Of course, I read all of my students' compositions, and I enjoy helping writers master their craft. However, when I come across a well-written introduction that grabs my attention, I inwardly rejoice and look forward to reading on. You will have to exercise caution and consider your audience when you think about how you will introduce your essay. English teachers will probably like most of the techniques I'll present here, but you will need to use discernment when writing in other subject areas.

When you write your introduction, make it perform two functions:

➢ **Grab the reader's attention.** Your essay has to compete with hundreds for the reader's time. When you include some item of interest, sometimes called a *hook*, you hope to compel the reader to continue reading.

➢ **Introduce your limited topic** and give some idea of how you will handle it. This helps the reader bring any personal experience to the forefront of his memory, enabling him to interact with your thoughts and words.

Additionally, an introduction might give some definitions, especially for unfamiliar terms, offer attributions (book title and author) for a literary analysis, or present some background. Above all, it must provide a smooth transition to the main part of your paper.

Kinds of Introductions
Although many techniques can profitably introduce essays, writers generally use the following:
1. Give background and introduce the thesis (also called the *funnel*).
2. Ask a question.
3. Show a benefit to be gained.
4. Begin with an unexpected, humorous, or startling statement.
5. Begin with a quotation or a familiar saying.
6. Begin with dialogue—real or imagined.
7. Relate a story or paint a descriptive picture.

Examples of each of these techniques appear on the following pages.

Dramatic Openings

Sometimes you might want to write an opening to appear just before your "real" introduction. A dramatic opening serves to engage the reader and make him want to continue. Borrowing a technique from screenwriters, the dramatic opening begins in the middle of the action like a movie or television show. The paragraph following the dramatic introduction falls back and picks up the essay's topic. Again, you will need to consider your audience when deciding whether or not to use a dramatic opening.

For example, the dramatic opening below served this student well in her essay on the mutualism between the fig plant and fig wasp, while the second paragraph introduced the topic and thesis (underlined). The student wrote this essay for her English class. Her science teacher might have felt compelled to note that fig wasps don't think.

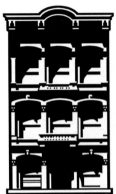

Like a façade, a dramatic opening gives your paper a "false front" to capture interest. The next paragraph can be a bit more sedate.

Suddenly a smell attracts the wasp. What is that smell? The wasp flies to investigate. Behold a fig tree, exactly what the mother wasp has been searching for. Flying through an opening on the plant, she sacrifices her wings, but she must get inside this fig. Even if it means her death, so be it. Searching, searching, then it appears. Spying a short style flower, she lays her eggs, then death consumes her. Her corpse rots away to nothing, but her children are safe and ready to enter adulthood when they hatch.

In the mutualism, or partnership, between a specific fig tree and its helper the fig wasp, neither creature can survive without the other. While the wasp needs a place to lay its eggs, the fig needs something to deliver pollen and provide it with nutrients so it can reproduce. In this specific partnership, neither the fig nor its helper can survive on its own because they need each other; they were designed to work together. (from "The Grave Story of the Fig Wasp" by Amber Myers)

Here's another example of a dramatic opening. A few years ago I took a graduate level course from a university and studied how to teach students who were learning English. Frankly, I took a risk. I didn't know my professor that well, and I didn't know how this opening might be received. So, I followed it up with the dullest and most boring paragraph I could muster. I even included the dreaded words, "this paper will" in my thesis statement, something I never allow my students to do. The technique worked, and I got an A.

There's a war raging in California. Not in the streets or shores; it's in the schools. Not in the hallways or cafeterias; it's in the classrooms—the classrooms that teach English Language Learners. Presently, General Ron Unz holds the high ground after winning the Battle of Proposition 227 in 1998. However, the opposition, under the scattered leadership of Field Marshals Stephen Krashen and John Crawford, is marshalling its troops and seeking intelligence to overthrow the tyranny of sheltered English immersion and reinstate bilingual education. This war has already produced casualties: English Learners who finish their education unable to speak proficient English. Both sides blame the other for this travesty.

Prior to 1987, bilingual education was the law in California's public schools. When this law sunsetted in 1987, Governor George Deukmejian vetoed an attempt to extend it; yet over the next 22 years, the California Department of Education all but mandated bilingual education. This changed in 1998 with the passage of Proposition 227. This paper will examine the changes wrought by that addition to California's education code with an attempt to evaluate its effect on English Language Learners. (from "California's Language Wars" by Lesha Myers)

Problems with Introductions

Omitting Them

The most common problem with introductions is omitting them. Beginning writers often just start their paper with their first body paragraph. In biographies, the first line of a younger student's report will invariably say something like, "George Washington was born in 1732." Although fine for a beginning writer, you're not a beginning writer.

Jumping the Gun

Another problem with introductions is what I call "jumping the gun." Students start writing their essay in their introduction, before they get to the body. Anxious to provide their evidence, students jump in and present their arguments, statistics, or other support. Remember, the introduction serves to provide background and a hook. It serves a taste of what is to come. It doesn't serve the whole meal.

Uh... Dull

The other common problem with introductions is they tend to be boring. Although parents and teachers have to read their students' essays, there's no need to make the process painful. By expending some effort, you can make your essay's entrance more enjoyable and maybe improve your grade.

Creativity

On the exercises that follow, you will have a chance to learn and practice each of the introductory techniques. I want you to have fun with this and be inventive. English teachers really like creativity, and there is not as much opportunity to be imaginative in a essay as there is in other types of writing—poetry or short stories for example. However, also keep in mind that your creativity has to underlie and serve your purpose in writing your essay—you can't be creative just to be creative—and that your introduction naturally has to lead into and support your thesis statement.

Cautions

➢ Although English teachers love creativity, teachers of other subjects (especially science) may not. Know your audience.

➢ Unless you are relating personal experience that supports your arguments, do not use "I" or its cousins (me, my, our, etc.) in any form in your essay. Especially avoid "I think" (Who else would be thinking?), "I am going to" (Just do it!), or any similar phrases.

Types of Introductions

Excerpt of an Example
(Please note: Although these are complete introductions, in essays they can be and usually are longer.)

Description

1. Funnel .(Give background and introduce thesis.)

The introduction that gives background and introduces the thesis is the most straightforward. Usually it begins generally, then funnels the reader toward the thesis statement, a one-sentence encapsulation of the entire essay. Many newspapers and magazine articles use this technique, sometimes answering the five W's and the H (who, what, where, why, when, and how). Although these leads can be somewhat dry, they quickly let readers know the subject and focus of the essay.

In the last several years, scientists have accomplished an amazing feat. They have mapped the entire human genome. While making way for medical advances that might benefit millions, scientists have stumbled on some rocky moral issues. <u>Before scientists continue their research, those issues need to be addressed.</u>

(Essay would continue by identifying the moral issues and possibly offering solutions.)

2. Ask a question.

By asking a question, writers hope to pique readers' interest in their essay so they will continue reading. They ask a question when they want readers to identify with the essay's concerns or focus on a specific problem. A carefully worded question will cause the reader to respond mentally, "Yes, I've always wondered about that." Be careful of questions with negative answers. For example, if an essay begins with the question, "Do you like spiders?" many readers might silently answer, "No," and quit reading. On the other hand, writers might use a question designed to narrow their audience. If the spider essay would only be of value to people who like spiders, the question would work well.

Old history books, popular opinion, and modern teachers all consider George Washington one of the greatest men of all time. They applaud his honesty by repeating the cherry tree story. They recount his heroic deeds, such as crossing the Delaware River in the dead of winter. They speak reverently of his faith and how he prayed for the Lord's blessing before battles. <u>Who was this man really, and did he deserve all these accolades?</u>

(Essay would examine George Washington's accomplishments and reach a positive or negative conclusion.)

3. Show a benefit to be gained.

Words surround modern readers. With so many options and so little time, readers need to be selective. Why should they spend time reading your essay? Introductions that dangle a benefit to be gained will appeal to readers, especially if they suffer from the particular problem you will discuss. They show the reader "what's in it for them" if they spend their time with your essay.

<u>It takes only thirty minutes a day. It takes only thirty minutes to prolong your life, increase your stamina, and provide good health.</u> Plus, remember all those clothes stuck way back in the closet, back where the light of day never shines? They will fit again. Save your money and your health. Begin to exercise for just thirty minutes each day.

(Essay would address the three topics: prolonging life, increasing stamina, and providing good health.)

Types of Introductions

	Excerpt of an Example
Description	*(Please note: Although these are complete introductions, in essays they can be and usually are longer.)*

4.   *Begin with an unexpected, humorous, or startling statement.* Ha Ha Ha

Most writing follows an expected path. Sentences build upon each other to reach some sort of logical conclusion. An effective introductory technique breaks this pattern by offering something unusual and perhaps breaking down some natural resistance to the subject.

Would you like to read a really great book? One that changes your life? That challenges your intellect? That rivets your attention? <u>Then don't read this one!</u>

(Essay would offer reasons to convince reader to bypass the book.)

5.   *Begin with a quotation or familiar saying.* "To be? Or not to be?"

Introductions need to meet a reader where he is and pull him into the essay. Sometimes a quotation or familiar saying will provide a meeting place. Examples include quotations from literature, Bible verses, proverbs, or excerpts from well-known speeches. Authors use this technique to build a bridge to their own topic.

The proverb says, "A fool and his money are soon parted." I should have thought of that before I fell for Larry's get-rich-quick scheme. Next time something sounds too good to be true, I'm going to remember, it probably is.

(Essay might offer ways to identify and avoid an unwise business plan or offer suggestions for prudent investments.)

6.   *Begin with dialogue—real or imagined.* 66 99

In some ways related to technique five (above), this method repeats conversation. It might quote an actual conversation or create an imaginary one. It offers a friendly introduction to the essay's topics.

"Mom, I'm bored. Do you have anything I can do?" It sounded like an innocent question, but it started one of the greatest adventures of my life.

(Essay could discuss any number of fulfilling activities such as a ministry to the homeless, a new business venture, or a new skill.)

7.   *Relate a story or paint a descriptive picture.*

Readers enjoy stories. Essays that borrow elements of fictional writing can quickly capture readers' attention and gently lead them to more involved or controversial topics. The most effective essays that employ this introductory technique often return to it in the conclusion and finish the story. Humorous stories make this technique even more memorable.

As the announcer directed contestants to the starting line, I took a deep breath. Checking my shoelaces and running gear one last time, I confidently strode to my position. Although thousands of eyes watched me, I put them out of mind and asked the Lord for peace and stamina. Soon it was just me, the Lord, and the finish line.

(Essay might relate a personal narrative or transition to another theme.)

Notes

Use this page to take notes as your teacher directs.

Purpose & Function of Introductions

1.

2.

Kinds of Introductions

1. Funnel (background and thesis)

2. Ask a question

3. Show a benefit to be gained

4. Humorous, unexpected, or startling statement

5. Quotation or familiar saying
    www.thinkexist.com ¨ www.quotationspage.com ¨ wwwlquoteland.com ¨ www.brainyquote.com

6. Dialogue (real or imagined)

7. Anecdote (story)

Dramatic Openings and Closings

Potential Problems with Introductions

1.

2.

3.

Banned phrases:
"By reading this essay you . . . " or "I intend to show . . . " or "By way of introduction . . . " or "I . . . "

Introductions Modeling

1. Funnel

A Christian's speech must glorify the Lord at all times. Grace should season each sentence. Sometimes, however, Christians face tough situations. Sometimes they need to warn or confront. Sometimes they need to turn conversations around. Above all, Christians need to use their time wisely and not over commit themselves. They must learn to say "no" graciously.

Directions: The above introduction gives some background and states the thesis. Rewrite it using each of the following introductory techniques, and try to include other style techniques you have learned. Since this is an exercise and since you cannot ask questions, you may take liberties by inventing some imaginative details. Of course, when writing actual essays, fabricating details would be highly unethical.

2. Ask a question.

_____

_____

_____

_____

_____

_____

_____

_____

_____

3. Show a benefit to be gained.

_____

_____

_____

_____

_____

_____

_____

_____

_____

4.   Begin with an unexpected, humorous, or startling statement.

_____

_____

_____

_____

_____

_____

5.   Begin with a quotation or familiar saying.

_____

_____

_____

_____

_____

_____

6.   Begin with dialogue—real or imagined.

_____

_____

_____

_____

_____

_____

7.   Relate a story or paint a descriptive picture.

_____

_____

_____

_____

_____

_____

1.   Introduction

Local municipal gardens frequently search for volunteers to give tours of their facilities. In fact, the Bancroft Gardens in Walnut Creek will offer a training class next week. The eight-week program will equip docents to lead tours, identify plants and their origins, and use drought-tolerant plants in local gardens.

Directions: The above introduction gives some background and states the thesis. Rewrite it using each of the following introductory techniques, and try to include other style techniques you have learned. Since this is an exercise and since you cannot ask questions, you may take liberties by inventing some imaginative details. Of course, when writing actual essays, fabricating details would be highly unethical.

2.   Ask a question.

_____

_____

_____

_____

_____

_____

_____

_____

_____

3.   Show a benefit to be gained.

_____

_____

_____

_____

_____

_____

_____

_____

_____

_____

4.   Begin with an unexpected, humorous, or startling statement.

_____

_____

_____

_____

_____

5.   Begin with a quotation or familiar saying.

_____

_____

_____

_____

_____

6.   Begin with dialogue—real or imagined.

_____

_____

_____

_____

_____

7.   Relate a story or paint a descriptive picture.

_____

_____

_____

_____

_____

1.   Introduction

Inventions litter history and arose from necessity. Inventors saw a problem and devised a solution. The monks of the Middle Ages had a problem. To fulfill the obligation of Psalm 63:6, "When I remember thee upon my bed, and meditate on thee in the night watches," they needed a reliable way to awaken each night for monastic prayers. That necessity led to one of the greatest inventions of all time: the medieval mechanical clock. Now clocks are everywhere. <u>Providing a reliable way to tell time, clocks drastically impact society and all of life.</u>

Directions: The above introduction gives some background and states the thesis. Rewrite it using each of the following introductory techniques, and try to include other style techniques you have learned. Since this is an exercise and since you cannot ask questions, you may take liberties by inventing some imaginative details. Of course, when writing actual essays, fabricating details would be highly unethical.

2.   Ask a question.

_____

_____

_____

_____

_____

_____

_____

_____

3.   Show a benefit to be gained.

_____

_____

_____

_____

_____

_____

_____

_____

_____

4.   Begin with an unexpected, humorous, or startling statement.

_____

_____

_____

_____

_____

_____

5.   Begin with a quotation or familiar saying.

_____

_____

_____

_____

_____

_____

6.   Begin with dialogue—real or imagined.

_____

_____

_____

_____

_____

_____

7.   Relate a story or paint a descriptive picture.

_____

_____

_____

_____

_____

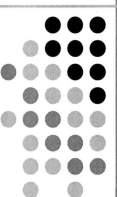

6 | CONCLUSIONS

Closings

Conclusions bring elegant essays to a satisfying end. At the final sentence, the reader must be content. He must not turn the page to look for more. Additionally, the conclusion should do the following:

1. Refrain from introducing any new information. If you want to discuss a new topic, add another body paragraph.
2. Make an application, or suggest a course of action based on information you have already discussed.
3. Emphasize the most important point or what you want the reader to remember.
4. Tie up any loose ends, and reward your reader for reading.

As the introduction draws readers into your topic, the conclusion should gently lead them back out. You might end with a judgment or an application of your main point.

Kinds of Conclusions
As with introductions, you may choose from several different types of concluding techniques. Ideally, you want to provide a frame for your essay and tie the introduction and conclusion together. Consequently, the type of conclusion you choose might depend on the introductory technique you used. These could be similar. For example, if you asked a question in the introduction, you might answer it in the conclusion. Examples of conclusions appear on the next page and include these:

1. Revisit (don't restate) the thesis and summarize the main topics.
2. Answer or ask a question.
3. Show the benefit gained.
4. End with an unexpected or humorous statement.
5. End with a suggested course of action.
6. End with a quotation or familiar saying.
7. Finish the story.

Dramatic Closings
If you began your essay with a dramatic opening, you might include a dramatic closing to bookend your paper. You may write most of your concluding paragraph using another technique, revisiting your major points, for example, but your conclusion might also include some kind of tie-in or reference back to your dramatic opening.

In the report on mutualism between the fig and fig wasp, excerpted in the section on introductions, the student included this reference in her conclusion:

> Although they may not realize it, when people eat figs they consume wasp corpses.

In my paper on teaching English language learners, I included this sentence in my conclusion:

> The battle has been won, but the war continues. Unfortunately, the causalities include too many English language learners.

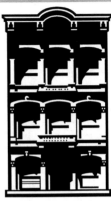

As your readers "exit" your essay, once again they should pass through your façade.

A Basic Pattern

Sometimes you aren't looking for a creative conclusion; you just want to end your essay. Still, you want it to be informative and compelling—it is your last word after all. Is there a pattern you can use when writing a basic conclusion? Yes, there is. It works this way:

1. **Revisit your thesis statement**. Begin by reminding your audience of your point, the position you want to argue, or the purpose of your essay. Do not restate your thesis, although you may repeat a word or two. Instead, reword it or refer to it in some way. Your purpose is to make your audience think, "Oh, yeah. This is the essay's focus." Do not make your audience think, "He just said this a minute ago."

   Thesis example: Watching too much television steals valuable time from other pursuits.

   Revisit: The time people spend watching television prevents them from participating in other activities.

2. **So what?** Remind your audience of your purpose, the reason you wrote the essay in the first place. Put yourself in the place of the reader and ask yourself, "So what? What have I learned? What should I remember? Why did I spend five (or ten) minutes of my life reading this essay?"

   A frequent "so what" is a call to action. You might want your audience to do something constructive.

   Example One: Turn Off Your TV Week is approaching. Consider joining the millions of people throughout the world who bury the remote control for a week and seek other interests.

   Example Two: Take better care of yourself; after all, you deserve it. Instead of joining millions of couch potatoes each evening, take a stroll around the block, or play tennis with your neighbors.

The Elegant Essay

3. **Finale.** You want to make sure your readers know you are done so that they don't turn the page and look for more. You can use one of the concluding techniques we've already discussed or anything that comes to mind that sounds "finished."

<u>Example One</u>: Who knows, you might discover a talent—maybe your inner artist.

<u>Example Two</u>: Plus, you'll save wear and tear on your couch.

Use this basic conclusion anytime you're stuck or when your audience would not appreciate the creativity that you might normally expend.

The above examples applied to a persuasive essay, but the pattern works the same for the narrative genre. Your thesis should appear in your introduction, usually your final line. Revisit that. For the "so what?" talk about the lesson you learned, what the experience taught you, or what you want others to know. Then conclude with a final line.

For the informative or expository essay, again revisit the thesis. For the "so what?" summarize your main points if the essay is long. Don't do this if your reader can read your essay in less than five minutes; otherwise he or she will think, "I just read this!" Alternatively, talk about or emphasize your main point before concluding with a final line. The broaden out technique also works very well with informative essays.

Problems with Conclusions

Omitting Them
As with introductions, the most common problem with conclusions is omitting them. The final body paragraph may finish with a closing thought rather than a separate paragraph wrapping up the whole essay. For example, a beginning writer might end a biography by informing the reader when the subject died. As with introductions, this might be acceptable for beginning students, but not for experienced writers like you.

Piling It On
Sometimes students come to the end of their essay, but they still have some wonderful evidence they would like to include. However, they have exceeded their page limit. Rather than omit the information, they throw it into their conclusion and pile on the details in a last-minute rush to finish. All this does is increase frustration, especially if they are good points. Your reader wants to hear more, but you just give him a glimpse. If your point is worth developing, include another body paragraph. If that is not possible, omit it.

Since the conclusion is the last thing the reader will consider, it must be well-crafted. Just as an unsatisfying ending to a movie or book will spoil the whole, an inadequate conclusion will detract from your essay and cause readers to discount your point. Give thought to this very important paragraph.

Finally, except in the rarest of exceptions, never ever begin your conclusion with the words "In conclusion." Your reader is at the end of your essay. What else would it be?

Types of Conclusions

Description	*Excerpt of an Example* *(Please note: Although these are complete conclusions, in essays they can be and frequently are longer.)*

1. Broaden out. (Revisit thesis and summarize main points.)

You may wish to revisit all of the topics in your paper, especially if it is long. If it is a short essay, less than three or four pages, resist this temptation. Although it might have taken you a long time to write the paper, it will take your reader only a few minutes to read it. The topics will be fresh in his or her mind. If you do decide to revisit your points, be sure to state them simply, and then end with a concluding thought or quotation.

Whatever job you do in the summer, remember to do it to the best of your ability, as unto the Lord. You will be rewarded. Your bank account will increase, your skills will develop, and you will gain satisfaction in helping a neighbor by performing a necessary service. Most of all, you will be rewarded by your heavenly Father with, "Well done, thou good and faithful servant."

(The three main body paragraphs on finances, skill enhancement, and ministry are summarized.)

2. Answer or ask a question.

If the introduction asked a question, it needs to be answered. The conclusion offers a good place to provide an answer. Restate the question, and then briefly summarize the proof or arguments from the body paragraphs.

Alternatively, you might ask your own question to allow your reader to continue thinking about your perspective. For example, "We need to consider, do we really want government control of health care?"

So does George Washington deserve the praise history books lavish on him? Most definitely. Not only were his deeds heroic, his faith sustaining, and his stature dignified, his character demonstrated one devoted to the glory of God. America received a great blessing when Washington agreed to serve as its first president. He was a great man.

3. Show the benefit gained.

Readers may have been attracted to the essay to discover the benefit they would accrue through reading and acting on advice offered. Refer to this benefit in the conclusion and highlight how it can be achieved. Make the reader feel time spent on the essay has been worthwhile.

Good health is worth thirty minutes a day. Not only will it save time and money, you will feel youthful and invigorated with energy to spare. So be brave. Update your wardrobe from the dark recess of your closet. Who knows? The outfits might be back in style.

4. End with an unexpected or humorous statement. Ha Ha Ha

If you make your reader smile, he will remember your point. You might take a familiar saying (like "All's well that ends well") and change it slightly ("All's well that just ends"). You might choose a play on words, a humorous anecdote or story, or even satire, if you use it carefully.

After that day, I've always taken time to read a product's directions for use. I'll always remember that, although the outside of hairspray and furniture polish containers look similar, the inside is quite different.

Types of Conclusions

Description

Excerpt of an Example
(Please note: Only part of the concluding paragraph is presented because of space limitations.)

5. *End with a suggested course of action.*

You had a reason for writing your essay—to either inform, describe, or persuade. The conclusion is a good place to suggest an application. Tell your readers what you want them to do with the knowledge you have just given them.

Hang around the track and the stable, the stadium and the rink. Observe closely. Interview in depth. Listen to old-timers. Ponder the changes. Write well.
(from "Sports" in *On Writing Well* by William Zinsser)

6. *End with a quotation or familiar saying.*

Conclusions need to bring readers out of the essay. Sometimes a quotation or familiar saying will provide a transition back to the world. Examples include quotes from people, literature, Bible verses, excerpts from well-known speeches, or proverbs.

My favorite definition of a careful writer comes from Joe DiMaggio, though he didn't know that was what he was defining. DiMaggio was the greatest player I ever saw, and nobody looked more relaxed. He covered vast distances in the outfield, moving in graceful strides, always arriving ahead of the ball, making the hardest catch look routine, and even when he was at bat, hitting the ball with tremendous power, he didn't appear to be exerting himself. I marveled at how effortless he looked because what he did could only be achieved by great daily effort. A reporter once asked him how he managed to play so well so consistently, and he said: "I always thought that there was at least one person in the stands who had never seen me play, and I didn't want to let him down."

(conclusion to *On Writing Well* by William Zinsser)

7. *Finish the story.*

If you began your paper with dialogue or a story, you might want to finish it in the conclusion. Not only will this satisfy readers' curiosity, it will help them to remember your point.

Even with my stumble around the first bend, I finished the race in second place. I felt humbled when the crowd cheered me more than the first place winner. That day I learned to persevere and to trust the Lord with my every moment.

Notes

Use this page to take notes as your teacher directs.

Purpose & Function of Conclusions
1.
2.
3.
4.

Kinds of Conclusions

1. Revisit (don't restate) thesis and summarize main topics.

2. Answer or ask a question.

3. Show the benefit gained.

4. End with an unexpected or humorous statement.

5. End with a quotation or familiar saying.
   www.thinkexist.com ¨ www.quotationspage.com ¨ wwwlquoteland.com ¨
   www.brainyquote.com

6. End with a suggested course of action.

7. Finish the story (anecdote).

Dramatic Closings

The Basic Pattern
1.

2.

3.

Potential Problems with Conclusions
1.

2.

Banned conclusion phrase: "_____ _____"

Creative Conclusions Modeling

1. Broaden out.

Without a doubt, it's hard to say "no." It's even harder to say it with grace. We need to remember the Lord gives us a certain number of hours each day. It's easy to fill up that time with too many activities and become overcommitted. We need to guard our time and remember that sometimes saying "no" honors the Lord.

Directions: Rewrite the above paragraph using each of the following concluding techniques, and try to include other style techniques you have learned.

2. Answer or ask a question.

_____

_____

_____

_____

_____

_____

_____

_____

3. Show the benefit gained.

_____

_____

_____

_____

_____

_____

_____

_____

4. End with an unexpected or humorous statement.

_____

_____

_____

_____

_____

_____

_____

5. End with a suggested course of action.

_____

_____

_____

_____

_____

_____

6. End with a quotation or familiar saying.

_____

_____

_____

_____

_____

_____

_____

7. Finish the story.

_____

_____

_____

_____

_____

_____

_____

Directions: In this exercise, you will practice the basic conclusion. Write a thesis statement, continue with a "so what?", and finish with a concluding line.

1. Topic: Video Games

Thesis:

_____

_____

So What?

_____

_____

_____

_____

Final Line:

_____

_____

2. Your own topic: _____

Thesis:

_____

_____

So What?

_____

_____

_____

_____

Final Line:

_____

_____

1.   Conclusion

In the ages since the Benedictine monks, clocks have made their mark on every area of society. With the invention of the marine chronometer, sailors could compute latitude and longitude. Trade flourished. With better navigation, missionaries could travel to isolated areas. Witnessing flourished. With the division of time into hours and minutes, appointments could be kept and contracts enforced. Business flourished. Clocks have impacted society more than any other invention. They have shaped modern life.

Directions: Rewrite the above paragraph using each of the following concluding techniques, and try to include other style techniques you have learned. Since this is an exercise and since you cannot ask questions, you may take liberties by inventing some imaginative details. Of course, when writing actual essays, fabricating details would be highly unethical.

2.   Answer or ask a question.

_____

_____

_____

_____

_____

_____

3.   Show the benefit gained.

_____

_____

_____

_____

_____

4.   End with an unexpected or humorous statement.

_____

_____

_____

_____

5. **End with a suggested course of action.**

_____

_____

_____

_____

_____

_____

_____

6. **End with a quotation or familiar saying.**

_____

_____

_____

_____

_____

_____

_____

7. **Finish the story.**

_____

_____

_____

_____

_____

_____

_____

1.   Conclusion

Television wastes children's valuable time, exposes them to unsavory situations, and encourages them to be sedate. It is harmful. Considering all of the other activities that children might pursue, watching television is a very poor alternative. It dulls the body, the mind, and the soul.

Directions: The above conclusion used the "broaden out" technique—it revisits the thesis and summarizes the essay's main points. Write a conclusion to an essay that discusses some aspect of television using the following concluding techniques, and try to include other style techniques you have learned. You may rewrite the above conclusion or create one of your own.

2.   Answer or ask a question.

_____

_____

_____

_____

_____

_____

3.   Show the benefit gained.

_____

_____

_____

_____

_____

4.   End with an unexpected or humorous statement.

_____

_____

_____

_____

_____

5. End with a suggested course of action.

_____

_____

_____

_____

_____

_____

_____

_____

6. End with a quotation or familiar saying.

_____

_____

_____

_____

_____

_____

_____

_____

7. Finish the story.

_____

_____

_____

_____

_____

_____

_____

_____

7 | FORM REVIEW

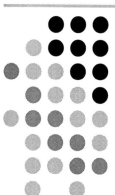

Essay Elements

All essays contain certain structural features. In previous lessons we have practiced these elements, which include the following:

1. **thesis statement**, usually in the introductory paragraph, to introduce your topic
2. **introductions** to attract your reader's attention
3. **body paragraphs** with convincing evidence that shows rather than tells
4. **conclusions** to provide a satisfying end to your thoughts
5. **transitions** between sentences and between paragraphs to move your reader's thoughts in your direction

Before you begin incorporating these elements into your own elegant essays on topics your teacher assigns, let's take a moment to revisit some of them. You won't need to practice body paragraphs with evidence because my examples will supply that, but you will need to practice the other four elements.

Bridge Transitions

Perhaps you remember when we talked about transitions that we practiced yellow line references and road sign connectors, but we ignored bridges or paragraph hooks. That's because up until this point, you've only written single paragraphs and have had nothing to connect your paragraph to. Now that changes. As you turn Charles Spurgeon's devotions into essays, make sure that one paragraph transitions into the next and that they are somehow hooked together. Refer to Chapter 4 if you need a refresher.

Notes

Use this page to take notes as your teacher directs.

Structural Features of Essays

1. thesis statement
2. introdutions
3. body pargraph
4. conclusion
5. transitions

Bridge Transitions

transition from one pargaft to the next pargaan

Directions: The devotion below was written in the nineteenth century by an English minister, Charles Spurgeon. Turn Spurgeon's devotion into an essay. Write an introduction (with thesis) and a conclusion. Separate the body into paragraphs and provide transitions. Look for repeated phrases or natural breaks and a topic for your conclusion. Give your essay a title.

"Wait on the Lord" (Psalm 27:14)

Sometimes it takes years of teaching before we learn to wait. It is much easier to forge ahead than to stand still. *althoo̧ğl* There are hours of perplexity when the most willing spirit, anxiously desirous to serve the Lord, *But* does not know what path to take. Then what will it do? Fly back in cowardice, turn to the right hand in fear, or rush forward in presumption? No, it must simply wait. Wait in prayer, however. Call on God and spread the case before Him. Tell Him your difficulty and plead His promise of aid. In dilemmas between one duty and another, it is sweet to be humble as a child and wait with simplicity of soul on the Lord. It is sure to be well with us when we are heavily willing to be guided by the will of God. But wait in faith. Express your unstaggering confidence in Him. Unfaithful, untrusting waiting is an insult to the Lord. Believe that He will come at the right time. The vision will come and will not tarry. Wait in quiet patience, not rebelling because you are under the affliction, but blessing your God for it. Never murmur as the children of Israel did against Moses. Never wish you could go back to the world again, but accept the case as it is and put it, without any self-will, into the hand of your covenant God, saying, "Now, Lord, not my will, but Yours be done. I do not know what to do. But I will wait until You drive back my foes. I will wait, for my heart is fixed on You alone, O God, and my spirit waits for You in the full conviction that You will be my joy and my salvation, my refuge and my strong tower."

(From *Morning and Evening* by Charles Spurgeon, August 30th.)

Name: _____   Date: _____

Class: _____   Exercise 12: Essay Form Review

_____

_____

_____

_____

_____

_____

_____

_____

_____

_____

_____

_____

_____

_____

_____

_____

_____

_____

_____

_____

_____

_____

_____

_____

_____

_____

_____

_____

Directions: The devotion below was written in the nineteenth century by an English minister, Charles Spurgeon. Turn Spurgeon's devotion into an essay. Write an introduction (with thesis) and a conclusion. Separate the body into paragraphs and provide transitions. Look for repeated phrases or natural breaks and a topic for your conclusion. Give your essay a title.

"His fruit was sweet to my taste" (Song of Solomon 2:3)

Faith, in the Scripture, is spoken of as pertaining to all the senses. It is hearing. "Hear, and your soul shall live" (Isaiah 55:3). One of the first performances of faith is hearing. We hear the voice of God, not with the outward ear alone, but with the inward ear. We hear it as God's Word, and we believe it to be so; that is the "hearing" of faith. Then our mind looks on the truth as it is presented to us; that is to say, we understand it; we perceive its meaning. This is sight. "Unto them that look for him shall he appear the second time without sin unto salvation" (Hebrews 9:28). We begin to admire it and find how fragrant it is; that is faith in its "smell." Faith is smelling. "All thy garments smell of myrrh, aloes, and cassia" (Psalm 45:8). Then we appropriate the mercies which are prepared for us in Christ; that is faith in its touch. By faith the woman came behind and touched the hem of Christ's garment, and by this we handle the things of the good word of life. Faith is equally the spirit's taste. "How sweet are thy words to my taste! yea, sweeter than honey to my lips" (Psalm 119:103). "Except ye eat the flesh of the Son of man, and drink his blood, ye have no life in you" (John 6:53). That which gives true enjoyment is the aspect of faith wherein Christ is received into us and made to be the food of our souls. It is then we sit under His shadow with great delight and find His fruit sweet to our taste.

(From *Morning and Evening* by Charles Spurgeon, August 25th.)

_____

_____

_____

_____

_____

_____

_____

_____

_____

_____

_____

_____

_____

_____

_____

_____

_____

_____

_____

_____

_____

_____

_____

_____

_____

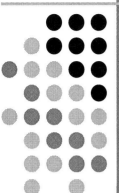

8 | THESIS & OUTLINES

Now that you've had some exposure to thesis statements and have worked with them a bit, I'd like to return to this topic and offer some refinement. Not only will this section help you to polish up your thesis statements, it will also help you organize your thoughts. These are our last two topics before we begin writing elegant essays.

Thesis Polishing

Universals, Superlatives, and Hyperbole

While creating thesis statements, be aware of some traps that some of my students have tripped over. You should avoid all three.

➢ The first is using a *universal* in the thesis statement, such as the words *all*, *every*, or *none*. Although in rare cases a universal might be appropriate in an assertion (such as according to Romans 3:23, "All have sinned and fall short of the glory of God"), at other times it might perpetrate a stereotype (All blondes have more fun.) or be considered insulting or even racist. Carefully consider the use of a universal in your thesis statement.

➢ The second issue is including a *superlative* such as *best* or *worst*. These words are hard to define and are subject to an individual's opinion. Especially in a persuasive essay, thesis statements containing superlatives will be difficult to support.

➢ Finally, avoid *hyperbole* or exaggeration. Don't make a sweeping statement such as, "Unless voters elect Mr. Perfect Politician president, the country is doomed." Although hyperbole might be useful to emphasize a point, in a thesis statement it generally serves as a distraction rather than an argument.

All of these distract readers and weaken thesis statements. Make sure yours don't suffer from them.

Clausal Thesis Statements

Generally, the thesis statement should not express two opposite or contradictory ideas. For example, the same essay should not make an argument both for and against capital punishment. On the other hand, some essay formats require you to examine two sides of a question and reach a conclusion. The thesis statement for this type of an essay calls for a clausal word such as *when, while, where, as, since, if,* or *although.* (www.asia)

➢ Although some consider it cruel, capital punishment discourages crime and establishes safe communities.

Clausal thesis statements also work well with cause and effect essays. When you are asked to identify both a problem and the issues that led to the problem, a clausal thesis statement is a good way to provide organization.

> ➢ If the founding fathers had tackled the thorny issue of slavery at the time they wrote the Constitution, the country might have avoided a bloody and divisive civil war.

History essays usually call for clausal thesis statements because most issues may be considered from alternative viewpoints. Including a clausal thesis gives the assurance that you have considered the question from an unbiased position.

Parallelism and Order

If a thesis statement contains more than one phrase, such as the three-pronged academic or working thesis discussed in a previous section, the phrases must employ a literary technique called *parallelism*. You may be familiar with this term from your geometry studies where it describes lines going in the same direction. In grammar, it describes phrases that have similar construction, that move in the same direction.

> ➢ If the first phrase begins with a past tense verb and contains a prepositional phrase, all phrases must be constructed in the same way: Golf <u>originated</u> *in Scotland*, <u>moved</u> *to England*, and <u>hit</u> its swing *in America*.
>
> ➢ The phrases do not have to be constructed exactly the same to be considered parallel. For example: Daytime curfews <u>infringe</u> on the freedom of minors, <u>waste</u> taxpayers' money, and <u>prove</u> ineffective. Although the first phrase contains a prepositional phrase (of minors), the second contains a direct object (taxpayer's money), and the third contains a predicate adjective (ineffective). However, all three phrases are parallel because they begin with a present tense verb.

Any construction is acceptable as long as all the phrases are parallel.

Since thesis statements provide a framework for readers, it is important that topics in your thesis statement appear in the same order as you discuss them in your essay. In the golf example, your essay would begin with a discussion of golf's beginnings in Scotland, then move on to how it developed in England, and finish with the contribution of America. Because your thesis places "hooks" in your readers' brains and establishes a place where they can hang your ideas, it's important that the hooks be set in the proper order.

Style

Since the thesis statement is so short, just one sentence, it should be powerful and memorable and have a little zip. It should have *style*. Three ways to give your thesis statement style are to use active verbs, strong word choices, and careful alliteration.

When beginning writers craft their first thesis statements, invariably they include a state of being verb, sometimes called a linking verb. You should memorize these words, and then banish them from your thesis vocabulary. State of being verbs include: *is, am, are, was, were, be, being,* and *been.* Which thesis statement sounds more powerful to you?

> ➢ Eating fast food is unhealthy.
> ➢ Fast food clogs blood vessels and causes disease.

The Elegant Essay

In addition to banishing state-of-being verbs, look for ways to bring your word choices alive. Use your thesaurus or *Synonym Finder* to look for the freshest words. Since your thesis statement is the cornerstone of your essay, you can afford to put more effort into it than you might into the rest of your paper:

> ➢ Fast food clogs arteries and destroys lives.

Finally, alliteration, the repetition of initial consonant sounds in words, might add interest and punch to a thesis statement, although it can be overdone:

> ➢ Fast food fills physiques with fat.

You will need to use alliteration carefully. English teachers will probably love it, history teachers might, and science teachers will probably think it sounds funny.

Answering Prompts

Often teachers will ask students to answer a specific question or write about a defined topic. The question or topic is the *prompt*. A common technique is either to ask a question or to make a statement and then ask for a persuasive essay that agrees, disagrees, or qualifies the statement. To illustrate this process, let's consider the following prompt:

> ➢ Is the Internet a hero or a villain?

You might be tempted just to answer the question: The Internet is a hero. However, not only does this thesis contain a state-of-being verb, it exhibits other weaknesses.

The Questions

To test whether or not you have written a good thesis statement, ask yourself these questions:

1. **Does the thesis answer the prompt?** "The Internet is a hero" technically addresses the prompt, but only superficially. It should be expanded. As you work on the wording, another problem might arise: You might find that you have wandered away from the prompt. When you get an acceptable working or draft thesis statement, re-read the prompt to be sure you have addressed it.

2. **Does it take a specific position?** In a persuasive essay, you must make a claim or an argument. Your thesis should create a dividing line with views on both sides. A thesis such as "Most American households have Internet access today" is not a claim. It is a fact. No one is going to argue against this statement because it is a true piece of information, not an argument. "The Internet is a hero" does take a position, but it is a very weak position.

3. **Does it pass the *how* or *why* test?** If the first question your reader thinks of is

"how?" or "why?" your thesis needs work. Most thesis statements that include a state-of-being verb will be too vague, such as "The Internet is a hero." How is it a hero? To tighten up your claim, think to yourself, "The Internet is a hero because _____." It might take a couple of tries before you come to a working thesis. For example, if you say, "The Internet is a hero because of the many things it can do," you still need to ask yourself more questions: "What things?"

4. **Does it provide enough focus?** You can only spend so much time on your composition assignment. You have other things to do with your life. Therefore, your thesis statement needs to be narrow enough to allow you to discuss your topic in the amount of space you have allotted. If you contend that the Internet is a hero, you do not need to list all of its benefits. Instead, narrow the field of benefits—business benefits or communication benefits, for example.

Thesis Statements that Qualify

Above, I mentioned that sometimes teachers will make a statement and then ask you to agree, disagree, or qualify it. What does *qualify* mean? If means to limit the position, to assert that it is true only under certain conditions or in certain situations. For example:

> ➢ When used along with careful supervision, the Internet greatly aids education.

Instead of saying that the Internet aids education all of the time in every situation, this thesis statement limits its usefulness to only those areas that include adult supervision. Here's another:

> ➢ Turning off the TV promotes healthy lifestyles, but only when replaced with an activity that doesn't occur on the couch.

Qualifying thesis statements demonstrate careful thinking because they anticipate the audience's objections and deal with them immediately. Also, they build trust and make the audience feel that you have thought about all aspects of a topic rather than jumped to a quick or superficial conclusion.

Planning

I have two more tools to help you write elegant essays—some organizational tools. Both are planning charts to help you visualize what you will say and how you will say it. You probably are familiar with the traditional Roman numeral outline and may have used it to organize your thoughts. If it works for you, great!

However, some of my students do better with an alternative such as graphic organizers. My students have benefited from the two charts on the following pages.

Essay Planning Chart

The Essay Planning Chart lets you look at your essay globally. It includes all of the elements we discuss in this course as well as a place to note the key words and concepts you want to include in each paragraph. Use the chart to think through your essay's structure and content. You might also use the Essay Planning Chart to revisit your essay once you've completed your rough draft. Beginning with a new blank chart, outline your essay, and check to make sure you have all necessary elements.

Fill-In-the-Blanks Outline

The second chart helps you think about the order of your essay and how you will incorporate elegant essay writing techniques, such as how to begin, how to conclude, what points to include in the body of your writing, and most importantly, how to back those points up with evidence, or *showing* as I've called it. This form also helps you to keep track of your research.

Your Turn

It's time to practice. In the next two sections I will walk you through two prompts. One asks you to describe a person, which will allow you to practice descriptive writing. The other asks you to consider the above question: Is the Internet a hero or a villain? Both of these assignments will equip you to write elegant essays.

Notes

Use this page to take notes as your teacher directs.

Thesis Issues to Avoid
1. Universals:

2. Superlatives:

3. Hyperbole:

Clausal Theses
(www.asia)

Order and Parallelism

Style

Thesis evaluation questions
1.

2.

3.

4.

Thesis Statements that Qualify

Planning

The Elegant Essay

Modeling Thesis Statements

Directions: Please rate the following thesis statements using this rating system:
★ Amazing!   ☺ Excellent   √ Good   ?? Lacking

1. TV shows are always terrible.

2. There were inconsistencies in the story line because the writers were on strike.

3. Entertainment is a mind-numbing drug that people use to run away from the world.

4. There were many kinds of programs on the Discovery Channel.

5. TV is bad, bold, brazen, and boring.

6. Movies are usually violent because so many murders and car crashes happen in them.

7. TV shows would be better if producers focused on three things: using less violence, showing less flesh, and to make their writers work harder.

8. In our society, everyone blames entertainment for destroying the morals and minds of youth, but in actuality entertainment is merely a scapegoat for others' failures.

9. By touting equality, television builds unity and understanding within communities.

10. Television promotes communication and compassion by exposing society to a variety of common situations.

11. When viewed with discernment, television programs create a smaller and more cohesive world by encouraging people to care and share.

TV Topic Thesis Workshop

Directions: Please rate the following thesis statements using this rating system:
★ Amazing!   ☺ Excellent   √ Good   ?? Lacking

What, if anything, does the thesis statement lack? How would you change it?

☺ 1. From its excessive swearing to its graphic violence, *South Park* represents just one of the many shows on television that negatively influences children.

?? 2. Television has been proven to steal time away from more important activities.

√ 3. Watching too much TV can affect children in negative ways, such as causing childhood obesity, laziness, or even changing children to become violent.

4. TV is a major distraction to the children in this society and causes them to put off what they are supposed to do.

?? 5. Television creates a deceptive world that harms the lives of children.

6. Television negatively affects people by producing idle time, illusions about reality, and decreased health.

7. Because television causes obsession, exposes children to violence at a young age, and contains program content that can potentially harm children, it is unhealthy.

8. Even though there are several advantages to the television, there are many bad influences that are included.

9. Addiction to television will negatively influence children to lie, swear, and perform violent acts.

10. As a result, television's excessive sexual content poisons children's minds.

?? 11. Therefore, children's television should be limited because it harms them.

☺ 12. Television destroys a minor's adolescence in such a way that children learn violence, lose their innocence, and become less active.

13. The lives of adolescents today are directly influenced by the portrayal of women on TV.

Advertising Topic Thesis Workshop

Directions: Please rate the following thesis statements using this rating system:
★ Amazing!   ☺ Excellent   √ Good   ?? Lacking

What, if anything, does the thesis statement lack?
How would you change it?

1. Although there are some negative effects of advertising, advertising is generally good because it educates people, raises cultural awareness, and causes people to consider helping the world.

2. Advertising educates the public, informs viewers about their world, and encourages moral actions.

3. The effects of advertising are detrimental if they cause people to be selfish and greedy, but if they cause people to attend to the needs of others, the effects are beneficial.

4. Ultimately, advertising will bring about negative effects because it sells the wrong products and uses tricky techniques to deceive people into buying the items.

5. It has become blatantly evident that what we wear, what we say, and how we live are determined not by our own set of values but by a set of values instilled upon us by Corporate America.

6. Advertisements enable us to understand the world, and without them we would be devoid of the fundamental abilities of communication and understanding.

7. Not only do advertisements increase the convenience of daily life, they may also save lives or benefit those in need.

8. The invention of advertising is the best thing that has ever happened to our world.

9. Without advertising, many people would be obvious to changes in culture and would be left in the dark.

10. Advertisers aim for the hearts and minds of men and women, altering their perceptions to create a mentality of soulless commercialism.

11. Advertising enriches living because it informs people of the latest and greatest effective and time-saving products.

Directions: Using your choice of the graphic organizers presented in this chapter, outline the following essay.

It's a Slow News Day

Yesterday I was watching TV when I heard about a hippie doing something illegal. I thought to myself, "The hippies burn another hummer?" Well, I was wrong. It turned out someone had broken into a chicken farm and videotaped the poor conditions of chickens. Five to six chicken were stuffed in cages no larger than a microwave. The hippie was then sued for breaking into private property. The news reporters tried to make me care about poultry, but quite frankly, I do not care about chicken unless I am eating it. What on earth does this have to do with global warming? Well, global warming is just like that news article; it does not deserve coverage. The only reason it is a story is because it's a slow news day. There are no more continents, giant sea monsters, or new planets to be found, so attention-loving scientists have publicized the issue of global warming. I am not saying global warming is not happening, but I am saying we humans are not responsible for it and it is not a catastrophic problem. We do contribute emissions into the air, but that is a miniscule amount compared to other natural sources. Even if we wanted to further lower our release of greenhouse gases, it would be a serious mismanagement of priorities. The way we are approaching and planning to approach the global warming problem is completely backwards and wrong.

The Earth is an ancient complicated machine that we humans will probably never completely understand. Even with our big fancy computers and satellites, scientists have no real answer to how much of an effect greenhouse gases have on the Earth's overall temperature. We are, however, led to believe by these same computers that doomsday is approaching. The Earth will get hotter and hotter, the sea levels will rise and we will all drown; storms will be more numerous and severe; all living organisms and humans will all die from the extinction of vegetation. Do we really see this happening though? No, we do not. Environmentalists claim that the Earth's temperature has risen one degree Celsius in the last 100 years (Weisbrot). Guess what, it is still 20 times cooler than it was in the 18th century (Robinson). These same "scientists" claim that sea levels will rise by 50 cm by 2100 (Bjorn), but they seem to have forgotten that they have risen 10-25 centimeters just in the twentieth century alone (Bjorn). Did anyone notice this rise? Were the beaches of Miami and San Diego abandoned in fear of the rising sea level? No, they were not. But wait, scientists allege storms destroyed beaches, and those were caused by global warming. Admittedly, there have been super-storms like Katrina, but these storms are just part of Earth's natural cycle. Again the environmentalists do not mention the fact that the weather is so complicated that it is impossible to know whether global warming is the cause. How about the extinction of plants? Hotter weather means fewer plants, right? Wrong, again. Plants have adapted for thousands of years to their environments; a single degree in temperature change is nothing for them. In fact, carbon dioxide is great for plants—they need it. The more carbon there is, the better plants do. Forgetting facts that contradict their own opinions is a common strategy for these environmentalists, but who exactly are they?

These people are scientists with too much time on their hands. Instead of discovering new ways of producing energy, they find ways of scaring the general public so it will listen to them. Thirty years ago, these same people claimed that the world would freeze over. No one listened, so they changed their official position and said it was heating up. Then they put some models into the computer along with some faulty data. The computer predicted catastrophe. Preying on the public's trust in the new age of the computer, they then submitted these phony results as facts. They claimed we were adding too much carbon dioxide into the air.

Humans are not the only ones to add carbon into the air. Every living thing contains carbon, and once it dies it will release the carbon. Humans are responsible for only 3.225% percent of carbon dioxide emissions (Singer), and the rest of the 96.775% is caused by natural factors. There is absolutely nothing that we can do about that 97 percent, but we can reduce our contribution. In 1998, the Kyoto Protocol's signing began. Asking for countries to reduce carbon dioxide emissions by twenty-five percent, it would cost hundreds of billions of dollars per year (West). Wisely, the United States opted not to sign it. In fact, the Senate voted 95 to 0 against it and said that signing it "would result in serious harm to the economy of the United States" (West). The United States would not be the only country to suffer. Civilized countries all over the world would have colossal numbers of blackouts. Countries would return to the dark ages. No more manufacturing, no more big cities, and in brief, no more advancing technology for the human race. Even if every single country were to obey the Kyoto Protocol, we would only reduce carbon emissions by 0.035%. In short, abiding by the Kyoto Protocol would require spending trillions of dollars and result in the unnoticeable change of future temperatures. We could instead use that money on the real problems of our generation: AIDS, education, and our own social programs. Spending money on the global warming problem is a complete waste of money

Global warming is a problem that we neither created nor can fix. It is just part of Earth's natural cycles. Yes, we should exercise good stewardship over the earth's resources. No, we should not worry that we will burn, freeze, or drown. It is time to stop the hype and go look for another source of news on those slow news days. Maybe we should pay more attention to hippies and hummers. (Jason Cheung)

Works Cited

Bjorn, Lomborg. "Kyoto Protocol Misplaced Priorities." *The Jakarta Post*. 15 Feb.2005. Web. 2 Dec. 2006. <http://yaleglobal.yale.edu/display.article?id=5280>.

Robinson, Arthur. "Petition Project." *Oregon Institute of Science and Medicine*. 1998. Web. 2 Dec. 2006. <http://www.sitewave.net/pproject/s33p36.htm>.

Singer, Fred. "Water Vapor Rules the Greenhouse System." 10 Sep. 2001. Web. 2 Dec. 2006. <http://www.clearlight.com/~mhieb/WVFossils/greenhouse_data.html>.

Weisbrot, Chris. "How Real Is Global Warming?" Web. 2 Dec. 2006. <http://www.thehcf.org/emaila1.html>.

West, Larry. "Should the United States Ratify the Kyoto Protocol?" *About.com Environmental Issues*. Web. 2 Dec. 2006. <http://environment.about.com/od/kyotoprotocol/i/kyotoprotocol.htm>.

Note: Essays should be double-spaced according to MLA formatting rules. This one is single-spaced to save space. Additionally, the latest MLA citation guidelines do not require specific URLs; however, some teachers still like to see them.

Directions: Using your choice of the graphic organizers presented in this chapter, outline the following essay.

High and Dry Here and Now

On August 23, 2005, tragedy struck the Gulf Coast city of New Orleans. Hurricane Katrina came barreling in with its 125 mile per hour winds and completely overwhelmed the city's flood walls, leaving much of the city underwater. Besides the estimated eight-million-plus dollars in damages, on an even graver note, over two thousand lives were lost, due in part to the destruction and tragedy that came along with the Category 3 hurricane. However, much of the damage done could have been avoided only if the government had done more prior to the hurricane to prepare the city for such a disaster and if more citizens had heeded warnings and evacuated earlier. Similarly, if the people of California continue to do nothing to brace themselves for the disaster just looming over its horizon, it will face a similar fate to that of New Orleans. The massive amount of evidence supporting the advent of an impending water crisis will have devastating effects on California's economy and well being, effectively leaving it high and dry unless we do something about it here and now.

Some Californians ignorantly deny that California's water problems are serious, but the evidence supporting an impending disaster is overwhelming. If we take a quick look at the statistics, it's pretty obvious that we have a huge problem on our hands. First off, let's take a look at the Sacramento-San Joaquin River Delta. This natural estuary covers over 700 acres and provides water to over twenty-five million Californians ("Deteriorating Sacramento-San Joaquin Delta"). To put this into perspective, California's total population is somewhere around thirty-six million; that means that the delta alone helps meet the water needs of at least eighty percent of Californians. That shows just how important this delta is to the well being of the Golden State. Now with the advent of global warming and lower rainfall recently, there has been a decline in the native plants and animal species within the delta, which is throwing off its natural balance. Besides natural causes, humans also play a negative role: As we start to expand our neighborhoods into the delta region, we further disrupt the delicate balance. Like New Orleans, the delta has unreliable levees that if destroyed by an earthquake, which is very likely, can completely ruin the balance of the fresh delta water delta as salt water from San Francisco Bay gushes in. California's well-being quite literally hangs on a thread. Some people might argue that if the delta failed, we could turn to other locations as sources of water, perhaps the snowpack from the Sierras. However this is no longer an option as 2006 - 07 proved to be one of the driest winters on record for California. The water provided from the snowpack was only sixty-seven percent of normal (Steinhauer) or as much as ten to twenty inches lower than previous averages ("California's Drought"). California is in a serious water crisis, and there is no doubt about it.

Although a drought does not sound as daunting as a hurricane, its effects can be just as catastrophic. Farming would be hit hardest. As of September 2, 2008, the losses already suffered by California farmers due to the drought are estimated at $259.8 million. If farmers are not productive, Californians, not to mention the areas the state supplies, will starve. Some may suggest that if California cannot grow its own food, we could just get it from other states, but this would cost California massive amounts of money that it could not possibly afford. Also, as farmers struggle, they have to let go workers. Already, 2,000 people have lost their jobs (Wood). The economy weakens. Food grows scarce. People suffer.

Because the problem is severe, Californians have to play an active role in conserving water. The government under Arnold Schwarzenegger has already done the best it can to combat the current drought. For example, they have already passed bills to pay for better water storage and even decreased users' water allotment by twenty percent (Steinhauer). However, we can go even further by taking more proactive roles in saving water. Wise techniques include keeping our shower times to less than five minutes every day, which can amount to an incredible one thousand gallons of water saved every month. Also, shutting off the water when we brush our teeth can save four gallons a minute and two hundred gallons a week for a family of four. ("100 Water"). There are many, many techniques available; we just have to be willing to give them a shot.

Conclusive evidence that California indeed has a water emergency should prompt us, as citizens of this state, to act now or face the consequences. Hurricane Gustav hit New Orleans recently, but because of better preparations this time around, it weathered the storm relatively unharmed. Hopefully, we will not have to suffer dire consequences before taking action. Katrina left New Orleans deep in water; do we want this drought to leave us without any?

Works Cited

"100 Water Saving Tips." 2008. Water Use It Wisely. Web. 7 Oct. 2008.
    <http://www.wateruseitwisely.com/100ways/sw.shtml>.
"California's Drought." Department of Water Resources. 6 Oct. 2008. Web. 7 Oct. 2008.
    <http://www.water.ca.gov/drought/>.
"Deteriorating Sacramento-San Joaquin Delta." California's Water Crisis. 20 Jul. 2008. Web. 7 Oct.
    2008. <http://www.calwatercrisis.org/pdf/ACWA.WS.Delta%202007.pdf>.
"Record Drought." California's Water Crisis. 20 Jul. 2008. Web. 7 Oct. 2008.
    <http://www.calwatercrisis.org/pdf/ACWA.WS.RecordDrought%202007.pdf>.
Steinhauer, Jennifer. "Governor Declares Drought in California." *The New York Times*. 5 Jun. 2008.
    Web. 7 Oct. 2008.
    <http://www.nytimes.com/2008/06/05/us/05drought.html?n=Top/Reference/Times%20T
    opics/People/S/Schwarzenegger,%20Arnold>.
Wood, Daniel B. "Water Crisis Squeezes California's Economy." *The Christian Science Monitor*. 12 Sep.
    2007. Web. 7 Oct. 2008.. <http://www.csmonitor.com/2007/0912/
    p02s01-ussc.html>.

Note: Essays should be double-spaced according to MLA formatting rules. This one is single-spaced to save space. Additionally, the latest MLA citation guidelines do not require specific URLs; however, some teachers still like to see them.

Introduction Notes

Thesis: _____

Introduction: ☐ Funnel ☐ Asks a question ☐ Shows benefit ☐ Quotation/saying/startling statement ☐ Dialogue ☐ Tells a story
Thesis: ☐ Informs (states topic) ☐ Implied (suggests mood) ☐ Persuades (states position to defend)
☐ Academic (three themes with parallelism)

Theme or Topic One

☐ *Informative: Adds detail, explains and expands theme*
☐ *Persuasive: Gives reasons, evidence, examples and illustrations, or quotes*

☐*Clincher bridges to next topic*

Theme or Topic Two

☐ *Informative: Adds detail, explains and expands theme*
☐ *Persuasive: Gives reasons, evidence, examples and illustrations, or quotes*

☐*Clincher bridges to next topic*

Theme or Topic Three

☐ *Informative: Adds detail, explains and expands theme*
☐ *Persuasive: Gives reasons, evidence, examples and illustrations, or quotes*

☐*Clincher bridges to conclusion*

Checklist:
(From assignment directions)

☐ ☐ ☐ ☐ ☐ ☐ ☐

Conclusion Notes

Conclusion: ☐ Revisits thesis ☐ Answers question ☐ Shows benefit ☐ Humorous statement ☐ Supplies quote ☐ Suggests course of action ☐ Finishes story
Transition: ☐ Bridge transition from final body paragraph
Last Line: ☐ Includes title of essay

Frame?

Title: _____

Introduction

Attention-Getter: *Immediately captures the attention of the audience in a manner that is favorable to the topic.*

Techniques: funnel, ask a question, show a benefit, humorous or startling statement, quotation, dialogue, story/description

_____

_____

_____

Transition to thesis: *Provide 1 - 3 sentences that make a connection between the attention-getter or hook and the thesis.*

_____

_____

Thesis Statement: *What you intend to describe, explain, or persuade the audience to do or the position you intend to take on a well-defined question. Should be stated in one clear and concise sentence.*

_____

_____

_____

Body

i. First point or weakest argument and how it proves the thesis:

_____

_____

Evidence/Support/Showing:

_____

_____

_____

ii. Second point or next strongest argument and how it proves the thesis:

_____

_____

Evidence/Support/Showing:

_____

_____

_____

iii. Third point or strongest argument and how it proves the thesis:

_____

_____

_____

Evidence/Support/Showing:

_____

_____

_____

Conclusion

Revisit the thesis: *What have you proved?*

_____

_____

_____

Application of your arguments: *Be sure to tie back to your introduction.*

_____

_____

_____

_____

Final impact: *End your essay with a strong sense of finality that will make an emotional impact on the audience.*

Call to action, Paint a picture, Benefit gained, Why it matters—the "So what"

_____

_____

_____

_____

References

If you use sources, list references below:

_____

_____

_____

_____

_____

_____

_____

_____

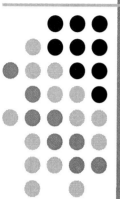

9 DESCRIPTIVE ESSAY

Descriptive Essay Practice

Are you ready? Ready to move out on your own and write your own elegant essay? In this section we will walk together as you write a descriptive essay, putting to use what you've learned.

Here's your first assignment:
➤ Describe a person.

Not much to go on, is it? That's where your brain comes in handy. You have to think of whom to describe and how to describe him or her. And, I have to warn you, often this first step is the hardest in the whole writing process. Remember, writing is thinking. It requires using that wonderful piece of grey matter that God created and stuck inside your skull.

Thinking

Three ways that I have found helpful to get my thoughts flowing are to ask myself some questions, do a free-write, and think using a cluster chart. Sometimes I use just one of these methods. At other times, I use all three: First I ask some questions, then I do a free-write, and then I make a cluster chart. Usually by then I have some good ideas about what to write.

Ask Questions
By asking questions, you are not only thinking about whom to describe, but what you might say about him or her. You might ask yourself questions like the following:
➤ Whom do you know well enough to describe? A friend, parent, sibling, teacher?
➤ What makes him or her unique?
➤ What character qualities does he possess?
➤ Why do you like to spend time with him?
➤ What kinds of things do you do together?
➤ What do you most admire about this person?
➤ Does he ever do things that are humorous? Strange? Frustrating?
➤ What is a special memory you share with this person?
➤ Pick one word to describe this person.
➤ Pick two more words to describe this person.
➤ You are recommending this person for a summer job. What will you say?
➤ You are recommending this person for a summer job. What will you *not* say?

Of course, you don't have to answer all of these questions. They are only meant to get your thoughts flowing.

One further comment before we continue. Your writing must be gracious. When thinking about the person you want to describe, you might think of some embarrassing moments. Think carefully. Should you write about them? If your friend read what you wrote, would he be offended, hurt, or humiliated? Before you even set pen to paper (or fingers to keyboard), decide that you will share what you write with your friend. This will help you season your words with grace. You might talk your assignment over with your subject, and if he or she is OK with the embarrassing moment, then go for it. He might also be able to help you think of things to write about and feel honored.

Free-writing

Free-writing is a thought dump. To produce a free-write, you will need paper, pen, and a timer. Set your timer for five minutes and write. The catch is that you *must* keep your pen moving. If you run out of thoughts, you still need to keep your pen moving, so you might have to resort to writing, "I'm stuck. I can't think of anything more to write." You will be surprised, though, because new thoughts will arise even as you are writing those words. A free-write might look like this:

> A person, a person. Well, Sarah is pretty unique. I like to spend time with her. She has a great sense of humor. I remember when we. . ., but no, I better not write about that. I think the thing I like most about Sarah is that she is thoughtful. Last year she was the only friend who remembered my birthday. She brought this huge bouquet of balloons and a card that said how much she treasured our friendship. I still have that card. Then there was the time that she stood up for me. We were on a field trip, and I tripped over a tree root and went sprawling. Some of the other kids started laughing at me and calling me a klutz, but Sarah came over, told them to knock it off, and helped me up. But the thing I like most about Sarah is, is, is, —

Thankfully, I was saved by the timer and didn't have to finish that last thought. However, my brain will keep working, and I will think of more things I like about my friend Sarah.

Remember, with a free-write your major objective is to get your thoughts flowing freely. Keep writing until the timer rings. Don't worry about grammar, punctuation, spelling, or even complete sentences. Don't erase. Just write. Just think.

Cluster Chart

Sometimes called a bubble chart, a cluster chart is a diagram that helps guide and stimulate thought. Let's say you have chosen to describe your father. Begin your chart with a central bubble and write an "is" statement, something like, "My dad is clever." Then ask yourself some questions: "How is my dad clever?" Or, "What makes my dad clever?" Or even, "Why do I think my dad is clever?" Draw spokes from your central bubble answering your questions. Be brief.

Continue asking your questions and drawing your spokes. Your goal is to end up with something like the chart on the following page. Remember, however, your chart should *never* look this neat. You aren't producing a work of art. You are thinking.

Cluster Chart Example

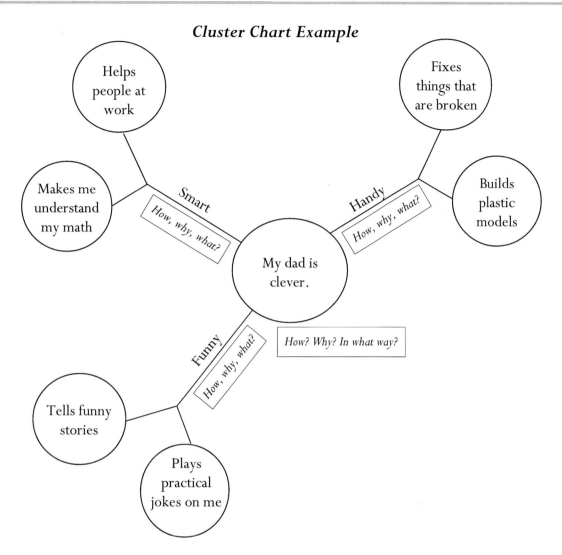

Developing Your Thesis

All the time that you are thinking about what to write, you should also be thinking of a possible thesis statement. "My dad is clever" is a thesis statement, but it is the kind a beginning writer would produce. It's OK, but just barely.

One way to find your thesis statement is to look over your questions (and answers), free-write, and cluster chart to see if you can find a controlling thought. A controlling thought is your most important idea or a one-sentence summary of the person you are describing. You probably won't be able to use all of your thoughts. Instead, you want to use what you feel is most significant. Think of it this way—your thesis statement should have two parts:

Your subject + your subject's importance

Thesis examples:

➤ Sarah puts others ahead of herself.

➤ My dad's humor brightens the day.

➤ Mrs. Mendoza inspires her students.

Remember, if you don't like your beginning thesis statement, you can always polish it later.

The Body

OK, you know your topic, that is, whom you will write about, and you have created a thesis statement or at least a working thesis statement. Now it's time to think about your essay's body. Because you have asked yourself several questions, completed a free-write, and/or drawn a cluster chart, you should have some preliminary ideas. Now it's time to expand them.

First, think of at least three details, sub-topics, themes, or areas you would like to write about. What do you want to say about your person? How might you reveal or convey your person's character? How will you make him or her come to life so that your reader will appreciate him as much as you do? Look back at your pre-writing, your thinking, for ideas.

One year I asked my beginning writing class to describe a person, and to my surprise, they all chose the same beloved science teacher. These were some of their topic ideas:

➢ Her faithfulness and Christian witness
➢ Her love for science and her ability to inspire her students to love it, too
➢ Some of her favorite and unusual expressions
➢ Her lab rules and her high regard for her students' safety

You will want to do the same with your person.

Once you have your topics, you will need to think about how you might *show* your ideas. What evidence, support, or proof do you have? When we discussed *showing* in essays, I shared a list of possibilities. As a reminder, these include the following:

➢ Example
➢ Personal experience
➢ Statistics
➢ Research/Testimony
➢ Observations
➢ Description
➢ Anecdote/Story
➢ Analogy

All of these can work with descriptive essays. To illustrate, I have chosen some examples from my students' writing about their favorite science teacher. However, I have changed her name and some details to protect her privacy.

Research

This student needed some additional information about his teacher, "Mrs. Swenson," so he interviewed her. Although students generally think of *research* as obtaining information from books, going directly to the source and asking fits within the category as well.

Mrs. Swenson says her love of science began early, with the encouragement of an elementary teacher who allowed her to work on independent projects. She continued to excel under the care of her instructors, and in high school, a teacher saved her from serious injury. While fixing a circuit, Mrs. Swenson's lab partner abruptly turned off the power without warning her. Frozen from the electrical shock, Mrs. Swenson stood helpless. Fortunately her teacher noticed and immediately struck her arm. The force of the blow sent her flying across the room, but it saved her. If her teacher had not noticed, Mrs. Swenson would have suffered third degree burns. In college, Mrs. Swenson's teachers continued to inspire her, and today she passes her enthusiasm on to her own students.

Example

Do you believe God answers prayer? Mrs. Swenson does. Continuously, she turns to God with her every need. Once during lab, a student lost a very tiny, but very critical, piece of equipment. For thirty minutes we searched in every corner, under all the desks, among the equipment, behind the books, and around the file cabinets, but we could not find the elusive component. Suddenly, Mrs. Swenson called a halt. She called for prayer. She asked the Lord to help us find the elusive component, and within twenty seconds, there it was. It was a lesson I will never forget. Mrs. Swenson begins all of her classes with prayer, but more than that, she relies on His strength at every moment throughout the day.

Description

You want to bring your person to life, and description will help you do that. You might describe your subject's physical appearance, or you might describe a setting. Science labs provide special sensory appeal.

Most science labs contain Bunsen burners, Petri dishes, and test tubes. Mrs. Swenson's science lab does, too. White lab coats hang on pegs above tubs filled with safety goggles, each labeled with the student's name. A locked cabinet contains chemicals that Mrs. Swenson vigilantly guards. Rows of plastic bins fill shelves, each marked according to category and contents. However, Mrs. Swenson's science lab isn't like most. Her lab isn't in a school; it's in her garage. The safety shower is attached to her built-in laundry tubs. The lab tables fold up and fit against the wall to make room for the family car. Students work under fluorescent shop lights attached to the rafters. During the fall and spring, Mrs. Swenson opens the garage door, and students spill out onto the driveway. The sun is bright, and the warm breeze dissipates the smell of ammonia or soldering. The winter is a different story. It's cold. It's so cold students wear two, three, or sometimes even four layers of clothing. Sometimes it's just too cold to work, and then Mrs. Swenson adjourns to her living room and supplies lectures and cups of hot chocolate.

Transitions

Once you have your body paragraphs, you need to make sure that one paragraph's thoughts flow into another's. You need to make sure you include transitions. Beginning writers might use road sign transition words such as *first*, *in addition*, or *on the other hand*. They work, but they are a bit formulaic. Don't forget to practice the bridge transition and hook your paragraphs together. To connect the description of Mrs. Swenson's early exposure to science to the prayer story, you might include this bridge:

> Mrs. Swenson's enthusiasm extends beyond science to faith. Do you believe in prayer?

To connect the description of the garage to a paragraph on teaching methods, you might begin with this transitional bridge:

> In hot summers or with hot chocolate, Mrs. Swenson is not afraid to tackle hot topics.

You don't want to make your transitions seem obvious or forced, but you also don't want to lose your reader. Remember, the purpose of a transition is to keep your readers' thoughts flowing along the same channels as your own.

Introduction & Conclusion

I find it easiest to write my introduction and conclusion together. Sometimes my introduction shows up during my thinking. There's a particular story or description or example that would work well. If I were to add a few sentences at the end of the above description of Mrs. Swenson's garage to introduce my thesis statement, it would work well as an introduction.

Introduction Example

If your person has a unique or unusual mannerism, you might use the *startling statement* or *dialogue* introductory technique like the following:

> "Oh, nostrils!" my piano teacher exclaimed.
>
> Nostrils?
>
> It seemed like a funny way to express frustration, but I was too startled to seek an explanation. Later when I knew her better, I asked her why she used this unique phrase. She told me that she didn't want to offend anyone with her speech and using the term *nostrils* seemed safe. It seemed strange to me, but in the years to come as she taught me to master the piano, it wasn't the strangest action she would perform.

Conclusion Example

Somewhere in your conclusion, usually at the beginning, you will want to revisit your thesis and the main focus of your essay. If you were not satisfied with your preliminary attempt to form a thesis, your thoughts might come together during this revisit. Additionally, remember that your conclusion should tie in with your introduction. For example, to conclude the above description of the piano teacher, you might say this:

Mrs. Moran brought me from "Twinkle Twinkle Little Star" to "Toccatina." She inspired me to excel. Her unusual teaching methods taught me to approach the piano with vigor, fortitude, and grace. I always remember the confidence she had in me. Whenever I hear the word *nostrils*, I smile.

Your Turn

Now it's time for you to give it a go. Write an essay describing a person using all of the techniques you have learned in this course. On the pages that follow, I've provided some planning charts to help you with the process.

Introduction Notes

Thesis: _____

Introduction: ☐ Funnel ☐ Asks a question ☐ Shows benefit ☐ Quotation/saying/startling statement ☐ Dialogue ☐ Tells a story

Thesis: ☐ Informs (states topic) ☐ Implied (suggests mood) ☐ Persuades (states position to defend)

☐ Academic (three themes with parallelism)

Checklist:
(From assignment directions)

☐ ☐ ☐ ☐ ☐ ☐ ☐

Theme or Topic One

☐ *Informative: Adds detail, explains and expands theme*

☐ *Persuasive: Gives reasons, evidence, examples and illustrations, or quotes*

☐ *Clincher bridges to next topic*

Theme or Topic Two

☐ *Informative: Adds detail, explains and expands theme*

☐ *Persuasive: Gives reasons, evidence, examples and illustrations, or quotes*

☐ *Clincher bridges to next topic*

Theme or Topic Three

☐ *Informative: Adds detail, explains and expands theme*

☐ *Persuasive: Gives reasons, evidence, examples and illustrations, or quotes*

☐ *Clincher bridges to conclusion*

Conclusion Notes

Conclusion: ☐ Revisits thesis ☐ Answers question ☐ Shows benefit ☐ Humorous statement ☐ Supplies quote ☐ Suggests course of action ☐ Finishes story

Transition: ☐ Bridge transition from final body paragraph

Last Line: ☐ Includes title of essay

Frame?

Name: _____   Date: _____

Class: _____   Elegant Essay Outline

Title: _____

Introduction

Attention-Getter: *Immediately captures the attention of the audience in a manner that is favorable to the topic.*

Techniques: funnel, ask a question, show a benefit, humorous or startling statement, quotation, dialogue, story/description

_____

_____

_____

Transition to thesis: *Provide 1 - 3 sentences that make a connection between the attention-getter or hook and the thesis.*

_____

_____

Thesis Statement: *What you intend to describe, explain, or persuade the audience to do or the position you intend to take on a well-defined question. Should be stated in one clear and concise sentence.*

_____

_____

_____

Body

i. First point or weakest argument and how it proves the thesis:

_____

_____

_____

Evidence/Support/Showing:

_____

_____

_____

ii. Second point or next strongest argument and how it proves the thesis:

_____

_____

_____

Evidence/Support/Showing:

_____

_____

_____

iii. Third point or strongest argument and how it proves the thesis:

_____

_____

_____

Evidence/Support/Showing:

_____

_____

_____

Conclusion

Revisit the thesis: *What have you proved?*

_____

_____

_____

Application of your arguments: *Be sure to tie back to your introduction.*

_____

_____

_____

_____

Final impact: *End your essay with a strong sense of finality that will make an emotional impact on the audience.*

Call to action, Paint a picture, Benefit gained, Why it matters—the "So what"

_____

_____

_____

_____

References

If you use sources, list references below:

_____

_____

_____

_____

_____

_____

_____

_____

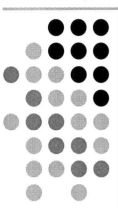

10 PERSUASIVE ESSAY

Persuasive Essay Practice

In our final lesson together we will practice the steps involved in writing a persuasive essay.

Here's the question you need to consider:
  ➢ Is the Internet a hero or a villain?

Each year the Lion's Club International sponsors a speech contest for high school students to compete for scholarships. The above prompt was the topic for the 69th annual Lion's Club International Student Speech Contest. Several of my students entered the competition and wrote very persuasive essays and speeches. In fact, this prompt was one of the most successful ones I've used while teaching writing because my students already knew a lot about the topic. They had plenty of personal experience and examples to draw on so that they didn't have to do too much extra research. Their essays were perceptive and persuasive.

Thinking

As with all essays, your first step will be to wear out and replace some grey cells. You might try asking some questions, doing a free-write, or drawing a cluster chart, but with a prompt that asks you to take a position, like this one, you might employ a T-Chart like the one below. Use it to think of arguments on both sides of the question.

Hero	Villain
Speeds communication	Spreads viruses
Enables research	Promotes scams and fraud
Saves lives	Enables phishing and identity theft
Advertises small businesses	Encourages rumors and urban legends
Makes shopping convenient	Distributes unsavory material
Connects people with like interests	Promotes addiction
Spreads worldwide news	Erodes privacy
Saves money	Encourages plagiarism

Developing Your Thesis

Once you've thought about both sides of the question, and maybe conducted some preliminary research, you need to state your argument in a thesis statement. Let's examine and evaluate several examples of thesis statements that address the prompt: Is the Internet a hero or a villain? Some of the good ones show the creativity of my students. Most of the bad ones I adapted to serve as examples.

Thesis Statement	Comments
Ever since it was invented, the Internet has greatly benefited people of all ages and all over the world.	Although this thesis contains a lot of words, it basically says, the Internet is good. How has it benefited people? Additionally, "was invented" is passive voice—something you should avoid—especially in thesis statements.
Society is improved because of the many opportunities presented by the Internet.	First, this thesis statement is not controversial and does not divide people into opposing camps. Second, it is not specific—what opportunities? How is society improved?
The Internet has drastically improved the lives of its users worldwide.	Without the adverbs and adjectives, this thesis basically says, "The Internet improves lives." How? In what way?
The Internet can be a hero or a villain depending on how it is used.	Although this statement is undoubtedly true, it doesn't make a good thesis statement because it doesn't make a claim. Instead, it sits right in the middle.
The Internet consumes vast amounts of time as it distracts people from their responsibilities.	Not bad. The position is clear, the topic is narrow, and I like the words *consumes* and *vast*.
Providing a service to society, the Internet allows people to vent their frustrations in a safe way.	Not only is this a tightly focused thesis statement, it provides an unusual response to the prompt that piques my interest.
Because the Internet allows people to act anonymously, it encourages crime and dependency.	Again, something interesting and out of the ordinary. It promises to make me think.
The abuse of the Internet has paved the path to sluggishness, crime, and sleaze.	Oh, yes! Look at those great word choices.
The misuse of the Internet has resulted in this great power becoming a catalyst for lust, loot, and life loss.	Tight focus and, what can I say? This English teacher *likes* alliteration!

Consider the prompt: Is the Internet a hero or a villain? Take a side and develop a thesis statement for each of the following areas:

1. Socialization/communication

_____

_____

_____

_____

2. Commerce/shopping/business opportunities

_____

_____

_____

_____

3. Inappropriate content

_____

_____

_____

_____

4. Education

_____

_____

_____

_____

5. Your own idea

_____

_____

_____

The Body

The body paragraphs of your Internet essay will build persuasive arguments to defend or prove your thesis statement. You might have to do some research to find evidence and support. Since we've already discussed several examples of how you might use the eight different kinds of evidence, support, or *showing*, I'd like to focus on *research*—specifically, how to use it correctly without committing plagiarism.

Plagiarism

Plagiarism, claiming another's words or thoughts as your own, is easier than ever, thanks to the Internet. It's stealing. Don't do it. Not only is it unethical, wrong, and dishonest, it's dangerous. At most schools, students who plagiarize, even unintentionally, suffer severe consequences. At best, they receive an F on their assignment. At worst, they are expelled from the course and sometimes even the school. I have a friend, a college professor, who faces plagiarism problems every semester. Since she employs a zero tolerance policy towards students who cheat, each semester she has to expel at least one student from her classes. There is no appeal. Don't even think about plagiarizing. On the other hand, you can ethically benefit from and use another's research and insights. In the examples that follow, I'll show you how.

Research

One of my favorite pro-Internet arguments relates the story of Bev Holzrichter, who claims the Internet saved her life. One of my students wrote about her as follows:

> Rapid communication on the Internet becomes more popular every day. In the United States, almost half of the population use their email daily ("Email Marketing Statistics"). New inventions such as webcams, digital cameras that emit image sequences onto the Internet, impact people's lives. According to her story on CNN, a webcam saved 56-year-old Bev Holzrichter's life. Every foaling season, people around the world were allowed to witness the miracle of horses giving birth. Webcams posted in Holzrichter's barn instantly fed information onto her Web site, allowing curious individuals to obtain a first-hand experience. As she talked to a friend on her cell phone, Holzrichter approached a stable inhabited by a horse that had just given birth. Not knowing that another mare previously provoked the new mother by trying to steal her foal, Holzrichter entered the stall. Immediately and instinctively, the worried horse kicked Holzrichter three times. She was thrown to the ground and could not stand up. Holzrichter's friend and other webcam watchers around the world dialed 911. Amazingly, calls from Germany, France, and the United Kingdom reached the emergency crew in Charlotte, Iowa. Forty-five minutes later, they arrived and attended to Holzrichter's knee and leg injuries. When her experience was over, she testified, "I don't know what would have happened if it wasn't for the webcam. I damaged my knee and my leg very badly. My temperature had dropped and I was in body shock by the time help arrived" (Holzrichter). Thanks to her friend and online witnesses, Holzrichter's life was saved by the Internet's swift communicative highway. (Stephanie Chow)

Stephanie obtained information for this well-written paragraph from two sources, one a reference and the other a quotation. She references the article "Email Marketing Statistics" as the source of her statistic on email use, and since there is no author for this article, she includes the first three words of the title, in quotation marks and inside parenthesis, after her sentence. Stephanie also referenced a story that Holzrichter wrote for the CNN.com Web site and says, "According to her story on CNN. . ." as well as includes Holzrichter's name, the author, in parenthesis after the direct quotation. In either case, she accomplishes her purpose, which is to point the reader towards the correct entry in her Works Cited page (discussed below). As long as Stephanie, or any writer, is careful to cite her sources or state where she got her information, she will avoid the difficulties of plagiarism.

Works Cited

In addition to a reference in the body of the essay, either a direct quotation or a paraphrase, you will need to give more information about your source so that your readers can check your information and do more research or follow-up if they desire.

I used to spend copious amounts of time teaching students how to create correctly formatted MLA (Modern Language Association) references. No more. Now I point them to an online citation generator. Using these generators, students fill in the blanks with information from their source, click enter, and presto, the correctly formatted citation appears on their computer screen. Most of the time they will need to change the font to match their own preferences, and sometimes they will need to create a hanging indent.

The sources appear on a separate page in the essay, which contains the words "Works Cited" centered at the top. Stephanie's sources would appear on a new page and look like this:

Works Cited

"Email Marketing Statistics and Metrics." *EmailLabs*. 2005. Web. 24 Feb. 2006.

Holzrichter, Bev. "'The Internet is my hero, it saved my life'." *Technology*. Cable News Net-

work. 25 Oct. 2005. Web. 24 Feb. 2006.

NOTE: The MLA guidelines were updated in April 2009 and no longer require you to cite the URL. The word "Web." points people to an online source. However, your teacher may still require the Web address. If so, the citations would look like this:

"Email Marketing Statistics and Metrics." *EmailLabs*. 2005. Web. 24 Feb. 2006.

<http://www.emaillabs.com/resources_statistics.html>.

Holzrichter, Bev. "'The Internet is my hero, it saved my life'." *Technology*. Cable News Net-

work. 25 Oct. 2005. Web. 24 Feb. 2006. <http://www.cnn.com/2005/

TECH/09/21/bev.holzrichter/>.

MLA Citation Generators

To locate online MLA citation generators, check out the following links:

➢ http://www.noodletools.com/noodlebib/express.php (my favorite)
➢ http://citationmachine.net/
➢ http://21cif.com
➢ http://secondary.oslis.org/resources/cm/mlacitationss

You may find additional helps by typing "MLA citation generator" into a search engine. Of the four cites listed above, NoodleTools is the most comprehensive and detailed. It will serve you in college and beyond, while the others might be easier for middle school students.

Finally, for more information about MLA standards, check out the Purdue University OWL (Online Writing Lab) at http://owl.english.purdue.edu.

Introductions

Story or Anecdote

As I've said before, sometimes my introduction just shows up as I am thinking about what to write in my essay or while I'm doing research. The above story about Bev Holzrichter might have worked, or any other story that demonstrates the usefulness of the Internet, like this one:

> Mr. Graham Tarling was your ordinary guy. He lived in the British countryside, he loved soccer, he even volunteered in his youth soccer league. But Graham was also a cancer victim. His doctors told him he only had about 6 - 12 months to live. The only way to save his life would be an operation, an operation his doctors said would be too dangerous to perform, so they wouldn't do it. Graham didn't want to die just yet, but what could he do? One day, his daughter introduced him to the Internet, and she showed him how to use Google. Graham looked on the Internet for a doctor willing to save his life. Eventually, he found a kidney cancer expert in California who put him into contact with Dr. Andrew Novick. Dr. Novick agreed to do the operation, and a few weeks later, it was done. It was a success. Today, Graham is still alive and well, able to play with his grandkids, thanks in large part to the Internet ("Net Saves Cancer"). This situation demonstrates just one of the Internet's many unique qualities. Besides providing tons of information, it has also opened up communication. And because of this, it has become a welcome convenience for its users. (Daniel Fong)

The Works Cited entry for this source would look like this:

"Net 'Saves Cancer Victim's Life'." *BBC News*. 29 July 2000. Web. 24 Feb. 2006.

<http://news.bbc.co.uk/1/hi/health/856764.stm>.

Quotation

Although sometimes an idea for my introduction appears, at other times I have to go hunt for it. One technique that I like to use, and that I recommend to my students, is to begin with a quotation. Where to find quotations? Especially regarding the Internet? On the Internet, of course!

My favorite Web site for quotations is <u>ThinkExist.com</u>. Others cites exist (just type "Quotation" into a search engine to find them), but ThinkExist seems to have the broadest range of quotations, some of them quite humorous. When I typed "Internet" into the search bar at the top of the ThinkExist Web site, twelve pages of quotations appeared, including these gems:

➢ "There's a statistical theory that if you gave a million monkeys typewriters and set them to work, they'd eventually come up with the complete works of Shakespeare. Thanks to the Internet, we now know this isn't true" (Ian Hart).

➢ "The Internet is the most important single invention in the history of human communication since the invention of call waiting" (Dave Barry).

➢ "Hooked on Internet? Help is just a click away" (Anonymous). And yes, I had to think about this one.

➢ "Getting information from the Internet is like taking a drink from a fire hydrant" (Mitchell Kapor).

Any one of these quotations could be woven into an introduction or a conclusion in a persuasive essay regarding the Internet. Students would need to do some research to inform their readers who the author is, for example: Mitchell Kapor, President and Chair of the Open Source Applications Foundation says, "Getting information from the Internet is like taking a drink from a fire hydrant" (Kapor). A search engine will give information about the author.

Finally, if you use a quotation, you need an entry on your Works Cited page. This is why I like ThinkExist.com so much—it automatically generates the citation. When you find the quotation you like, click on the author's name which will bring you to another page with more quotations by that author. Your selection will be the first one on the list. Look for and click on the icon labeled "Cite" and ThinkExist.com will automatically generate a citation in MLA format. You only need to copy and paste it into your document, and then change the font and create a hanging indent.

Personal Experience

Most of my students, and probably you as well, have a lot of personal experience with the Internet. If it would help you persuade your audience, by all means, use it. This student used his personal experience to create his opening:

Game: World of Warcraft. Character Name: Icefingerz. Race: Male Troll. Class: Mage. Level: 60. Does any of this sound familiar to you? No, probably not. World of Warcraft is a computer game that falls under the genre of MMORPG, which is Massive Multiplayer Online Role Playing Game. It is basically the type of game where you are allowed to create a character within the realm created by the company and control his or her actions and speech. I used to be addicted to that game. If I told you that my total play time accumulated to over thirty-five days, would you believe me? If I told you I paid over $170 to play this game, would you believe me? Well, it's true. I spent over a month of my life sitting in front of my computer playing behind a blue troll that shot fireballs at other monsters. Looking back at all the time I spent playing this game, I feel deep regret for not spending my time doing something more constructive. The Internet has become such a prominent force in society today that everyone in America basically has access to it. It provides many possibilities for good in addition to an equal number of possibilities for bad. In general, the Internet could be a positive feature in society if we can find the healthy balance in not overusing it; however, in today's society the Internet has become a villain because it acts as a constant distraction that keeps people from their responsibilities and consumes their time. (Chris Lee)

Powerful, isn't it? It's powerful because it comes from Chris's own personal experience. His words ring with authenticity. Also, he correctly used the pronouns *you* and *your*, something many of my students misuse. Chris was speaking directly to his audience, which happened to be me, his teacher. And he was right. I had not heard of the things he discussed. Oftentimes my students use the pronouns *you* and *your* to refer to a person: "The program teaches you how to skateboard." Nope, that's not me. I'm not in the market for skateboard schooling.

Conclusions

In a persuasive essay, the conclusion is the last chance to persuade your readers that your arguments are convincing and reasonable. First, you want to remind your readers in a general way what you have argued by revisiting your thesis. You don't want to restate it word for word. Especially in a short essay, your readers will remember something they read only a few pages earlier. Instead, you want to restate your thoughts in different words. You may find that you have wandered away from your original thesis. No problem. This is the time to go back and change it. Finish your argument. Say why it's important and why your position has merit. Use one of the concluding techniques we've previously discussed; the same one that you used in your introduction might work. Then, end with a powerful statement that has some punch, a pithy quote, or a haunting question. Here Daniel's conclusion:

The Internet sounds good, right? It provides tons of information and opens up communication. What could be wrong with it? Some people charge that the Internet is a creation of the devil himself. Yet, if you blame the Internet, you do it a great injustice. You're saying to the criminals that it's not all your fault, the Internet's partly to blame, too. We can't say that. Do we put a bank safe in jail for a bank robbery? How come we aren't getting rid of the postal service because there are scams in the mail? Because they aren't responsible, the criminals are. They are the ones committing the crimes. The Internet's not responsible for them. But, you know what the Internet is responsible for? It's responsible for opening up communication in ways previously thought impossible. It's responsible for letting regular guys like you and me have the same information previously reserved for professors and grad students. And the Internet is responsible for letting a man in England communicate with someone as far away as California, saving that man's life. That's what the Internet is responsible for. As technology gets better and better, and more and more people use the Internet, the possibilities are limitless. The Internet has been, now is, and will continue to be a hero for all mankind.

Your Turn

It's your turn to write your own essay on the prompt, Internet: Hero or Villain? On the pages that follow, I've provided some planning charts and a checklist to help you format your Works Cited page. Happy writing!

Introduction Notes

Thesis: _____

Introduction: ☐ Funnel ☐ Asks a question ☐ Shows benefit ☐ Quotation/saying/startling statement ☐ Dialogue ☐ Tells a story

☐ Informs (states topic) ☐ Implied (suggests mood) ☐ Persuades (states position to defend)

Thesis: ☐ Academic (three themes with parallelism)

Theme or Topic One

☐ *Informative: Adds detail, explains and expands theme*

☐ *Persuasive: Gives reasons, evidence, examples and illustrations, or quotes*

☐*Clincher bridges to next topic*

Theme or Topic Two

☐ *Informative: Adds detail, explains and expands theme*

☐ *Persuasive: Gives reasons, evidence, examples and illustrations, or quotes*

☐*Clincher bridges to next topic*

Theme or Topic Three

☐ *Informative: Adds detail, explains and expands theme*

☐ *Persuasive: Gives reasons, evidence, examples and illustrations, or quotes*

☐*Clincher bridges to conclusion*

Checklist:
(From assignment directions)

☐
☐
☐
☐
☐
☐
☐

Frame?

Conclusion Notes

Conclusion: ☐ Revisits thesis ☐ Answers question ☐ Shows benefit ☐ Humorous statement ☐ Supplies quote ☐ Suggests course of action ☐ Finishes story

Transition: ☐ Bridge transition from final body paragraph

Last Line: ☐ Includes title of essay

Name: _____   Date: _____

Class: _____   Elegant Essay Outline

Title: _____

Introduction

Attention-Getter: *Immediately captures the attention of the audience in a manner that is favorable to the topic.*

Techniques: funnel, ask a question, show a benefit, humorous or startling statement, quotation, dialogue, story/description

_____

_____

_____

Transition to thesis: *Provide 1 - 3 sentences that make a connection between the attention-getter or hook and the thesis.*

_____

_____

Thesis Statement: *What you intend to describe, explain, or persuade the audience to do or the position you intend to take on a well-defined question. Should be stated in one clear and concise sentence.*

_____

_____

_____

Body

i.   First point or weakest argument and how it proves the thesis:

_____

_____

Evidence/Support/Showing:

_____

_____

_____

ii. Second point or next strongest argument and how it proves the thesis:

_____

_____

Evidence/Support/Showing:

_____

_____

_____

iii. Third point or strongest argument and how it proves the thesis:

_____

_____

_____

Evidence/Support/Showing:

_____

_____

_____

Conclusion

Revisit the thesis: *What have you proved?*

_____

_____

_____

Application of your arguments: *Be sure to tie back to your introduction.*

_____

_____

_____

_____

Final impact: *End your essay with a strong sense of finality that will make an emotional impact on the audience.*

Call to action, Paint a picture, Benefit gained, Why it matters—the "So what"

_____

_____

_____

_____

References

If you use sources, list references below:

_____

_____

_____

_____

_____

_____

_____

_____

Works Cited Checklist

☐ Times New Roman #12 font

☐ Works Cited title—centered, no underline, no Work Cited

☐ URLs broken at a slash (/)

☐ No extra spaces. Example "The Title " .

☐ All entries hanging indent

☐ All information present, including "Web." and "n.d." if no date (without quotation marks)

☐ Citations in alphabetical order

☐ Double-spacing with no extra lines between entries

☐ No hotlinks

☐ Only works cited or referenced in the essay appear on the Works Cited page

☐ All inline citations correspond to a citation on the Works Cited page

☐ Entries are not numbered

☐ Nothing should be in all capital letters, like THIS

☐ When citing two articles by the same author, cite them by title, not by last name. Be sure to put the title in quotation marks.

☐ When citing an article by two or three authors, name all of them and separate with a comma: (Smith, Johnson, and Nelson). For four or more authors, state the first one and follow by et al., like this: (Smith et al.). Follow by the page number if applicable as necessary, like this: (Smith et al. 35).

☐ For inline citations use author's last name when available (Myers) or first two or three words of the title, in quotation marks, when not ("Universal Benefits").

Moving On

Guess what? You have now learned most of what you need to know to write elegant essays. Does this mean you're done, you may rest on your laurels, you may turn off your brain? Sorry, but no. There's always more.

Remember our first discussion of elegant essays, way back in Chapter 1? We talked about how all essays comprise five areas: structure (organization), content (ideas), style, mechanics (conventions), and voice (personality). Go back and look at Chapter 1 if this isn't sounding familiar. This course has majored in structure and content, while touching on the other three areas only in passing.

Where do you go from here? I would suggest two routes:

1. First, practice what you have already learned. Your teacher will provide you with topics to consider, but I'd like to suggest you keep a journal, or a blog if you prefer. Free blog sites abound on the Internet, and you can set them up so that you don't have to share your thoughts with the general public. Use your blog or a journal to write snippets (thoughts, introduction ideas, sentences, quotes) or full essays. Be sure to write in full sentences. 2 many shortcuts make u lazy and wont help u IRL. And, for heaven's sakes, use your shift key to create capital letters!

2. Second, read. Read everything—books, newspaper articles, magazines, cereal boxes. When you find something that sounds really elegant, something you want to keep track of, record it in your blog or journal. You might want to record similes, analogies, imagery, passages, reflections, or revelations.

In addition to writing, I suggest you invest in some tools. My favorite writing tool is Rodale's *Synonym Finder*. Can't find the perfect word to use in a sentence? The *Synonym Finder* has choice upon choice. A new copy will cost about $15, but you may find a used copy on a used book Web site such as www.Bookfinder.com. The other tool is a grammar and punctuation handbook. I like Diana Hacker's *A Pocket Style Manual* because it is so easy to find exactly what I need. Unless you use an online citation generator, you'll need the latest edition of this book to learn to properly cite sources you use as references.

We've covered the structure of basic essays, but there are other formats (sometimes called *modes*), such as cause and effect, compare and contrast, advanced persuasive, reflective narrative, and many more. Look for opportunities to expand your knowledge of these forms because they will benefit you throughout your life.

Finally, check out the writing resources from the Institute for Excellence in Writing at excellenceinwriting.com. These are terrific.

It's time to part. I hope these lessons have equipped you to take up the calling God has for your life. I pray He might use them so that you may give a reason for the hope that lies within you. Many blessings,

Mrs. Myers

And whatever you do, whether in word or deed, do it all in the name of the Lord Jesus,
giving thanks to God the Father through him (Col. 3:17).

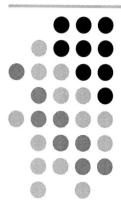

APPENDIX A

Teaching Models

Were you sick the day the teacher went over a particular model? Or were you present but a little out-of-it? Or did you miss a couple of things?

Never fear.

Models for all elegant essay lessons follow.

Chapter 2—Thesis Models

Essay Type	Topic	Slant/Details/Focus	Possible Thesis
Expository (Informative)	Friends	Loving the unlovable	Although it may be hard, creative friends can find ways to show love to those usually unappreciated.
		Overcoming shyness	With a little effort, shy people can learn to be comfortable around groups.
		Bible verses	The Bible says quite a bit about friends, especially in the book of Proverbs.
Narrative (Descriptive)	Holidays	Nostalgic	Paper ornaments, burning candles, and bustling kitchens highlighted the Christmas of Victorian times.
		Time for family	Battling traffic and crowds, families travel many miles to join each other in a festive Christmas celebration.
		Stressful/hectic	One year our family decided to spend the Christmas holiday in Hawaii; unfortunately, when we reached the airport, half the city joined us.
Persuasive	Television	Harmful	Unlimited television viewing can harm children.
		Wasteful	Watching too much television steals valuable time from other pursuits.
		Enjoyable	At the end of a weary day, television can refresh the mind and body.
Academic/ Informative	Career	Fulfilling Secure Profitable	Upon graduation, college students look for fulfilling, secure, and profitable careers.
Academic/ Persuasive	Smoking	Health Cost Image	Cigarette smoking damages a person's health, consumes a family's finances, and presents a poor image.

Chapter 3—Body Paragraph Models

<u>Essay Type</u>: Informative
<u>Support</u>: Personal Experience
<u>Thesis</u>: Gift-giving expresses affection and admiration.
<u>Body</u>:
When parents give gifts to their children, they send a special message of love. They say that they care in a very real way. One Christmas I wanted a computer with a special game station. I told my parents that I didn't want anything else, just the computer. My mom tried to explain to me that computers cost a lot of money and they just couldn't afford to buy me one. I insisted. In fact, I pouted. It was the computer or nothing. Christmas day arrived and I rushed to the tree. There it was! I was thrilled and played on it all day. Later, I asked my mom what present she received for Christmas. She said she didn't really need anything, and she and dad might go shopping during the after-Christmas sales. That's when I realized that both Mom and Dad had sacrificed their own gifts so that they could buy my computer. I felt guilty, but I also realized how much my mom and dad loved me. Their actions communicated their love.

<u>Other ideas:</u>
- ➢ **Example**: An example relates someone else's experience. Students could write about a time when their friend or someone in their family gave or received a meaning-filled gift.
- ➢ **Statistics**: A bit of Internet research might reveal the amount of money people spend on gifts, perhaps at Christmas time.
- ➢ **Observation**: Observations show reasoning and often include the words *might* or *could*. Students might observe that a small gift could accompany an apology and express regret.
- ➢ **Research**: Research in terms of expert testimony might be a little difficult for this topic. However, students might be able to research the origin of gift-giving and compare its original purpose to today's use.
- ➢ **Description**: In the example above, students might describe the computer or alternatively, the anticipation of rushing to the tree, tearing off the present's wrappings, and setting up the new station.
- ➢ **Anecdote/Story**: Although the above example relates personal experience, it also uses a story. Students could relate stories that happened to them or to others. For a Christmas story, students might retell the legend of the Little Drummer Boy or St. Nicholas.
- ➢ **Analogy**: Students might compare gifts to kind words. Both express love and affection. Your student might experience difficulty with analogies, comparing something known to explain something else. If so, return to them another time.

Chapter 4—Transitions Models

Put the following sentences in order; then add transitional words or phrases between sentences to form a complete paragraph. Do not change the substance of any sentence, although you may change the wording or structure.

1. One thousand students have taken advantage of this opportunity since it began in 1985.
2. "I've heard a lot of great feedback from the program. So many students are really glad they went," commented Dr. Thomas Johnson, the study's organizer.
3. For more information contact the university at 999-9999 or www.university.com.
4. Students can participate in other international study programs, including Brazil, Mexico, and Spain.
5. The London staff focuses on art, history, and humanities.
6. The course is challenging.
7. Students at the local university can earn the opportunity to study in London or Paris.
8. Time for field trips is included.

   This semester, students at the local university can earn the opportunity to study in London or Paris. In fact, one thousand students have taken advantage of this opportunity since it began in 1985. "I've heard a lot of great feedback from the program. So many students are really glad they went," commented Dr. Thomas Johnson, the study's organizer. The London staff focuses on art, history, and humanities, but students can also participate in other international study programs, including Brazil, Mexico, and Spain. The course is challenging; nevertheless, time for field trips is included. For more information, contact the university at 999-9999 or www.university.com.

Chapter 5—Introductions Models

1.   Funnel.

A Christian's speech must glorify the Lord at all times. Grace should season each sentence. Sometimes, however, Christians face tough situations. Sometimes they need to warn or confront. Sometimes they need to turn conversations around. Above all, Christians need to use their time wisely and not overcommit themselves. The must learn to say "no" graciously.

Directions: The above introduction gives some background and states the thesis. Rewrite it using each of the following introductory techniques, and try to include other style techniques you have learned.

2.   Ask a question.

Have you ever wanted to remove your foot from your mouth? Do you wish you could speak more kindly to others? Does your speech glorify God and show His love? As Christians, we are called to lead a life pleasing to God. This includes our speech. We must learn to speak courteously, exhort each other kindly, and say "no" graciously. (Samara Meahan)

3.   Show a benefit to be gained.

Christians have many opportunities to be godly examples to unbelievers. By taking heed of how we talk, we, as Christians, can control the conversations we are in. It is always important to be gracious no matter what. If we are talking to someone and they are not glorifying God, it is our responsibility to turn the conversation around. We must be able and willing to say "no" graciously. (Phoebe Pelot)

4.   Begin with an unexpected, humorous, or startling statement.

Mark Twain said, "It is better to keep your mouth shut and be taken for a fool than to open your mouth and remove all doubt." When we learn to control our tongues, we will not look, sound, or act like a fool. We will also be able to warn and confront, turn the conversation around when needed, and say "no" graciously. (Samara Meahan)

5.   Begin with a quotation or familiar saying.

Just say "no," but make sure that you say it graciously. Christians need to learn to treat people kindly and with respect. However, they also must learn to politely decline requests and not overcommit themselves. A Christian's speech should glorify the Lord at all times and grace ought to season each sentence they speak. Sometimes Christians face tough situations and must warn of confront. At other times they must change the subject to be sure that their conversations are pleasing to God. (Emily Turner)

6.   Begin with dialogue—real or imagined.

"Susie, you don't have time for another class! You're already taking gymnastics, piano, and tennis. You just don't have enough time in your day for all that you want to do."

"But Mom, I already said yes. It's not that I really want another commitment, I just couldn't say no. What can I do?"

Have you ever been stuck in a situation like Susie? Then perhaps you need to learn to say "no" graciously. (Brianna Swanson)

7.   Relate a story or paint a descriptive picture.

A lady sits on the sofa. Her head droops like a wilted flower. Her shoulders shake with suppressed sobs. "I can handle it! I can handle it!" she cries over and over to her cat. Had this lady learned to say no graciously, she wouldn't be teaching Sunday school, filling in at the nursery for someone who is sick, providing special music, and doing her regular nursery turn during the evening service. She needs to learn to say "no" graciously.

Chapter 6—Conclusions Models

Basic Conclusion

1.　　Narrative Topic: Friendship

Ever since my friend betrayed my trust, I've been more careful with whom I share my innermost thoughts. I think, if this friend shared these comments with everyone we know, would I be OK with that? Often I've stopped or waited until our relationship had stood several tests of loyalty. I've learned that sometimes silence is golden.

2.　　Persuasive Topic: Education

Attending college is incredibly expensive, but worth the investment. Planning ahead will lessen the burden as will exploring alternative methods such as online classes, self-study, and credit by exam. Do your research and consider your options. The greatest gift you can give yourself is to graduate debt-free.

Creative Conclusions

1.　　Broaden out.

Without a doubt, it's hard to say "no." It's even harder to say it with grace. We need to remember the Lord gives us a certain number of hours each day. It's easy to fill up that time with too many activities and become overcommitted. We need to guard our time and remember that sometimes saying "no" honors the Lord.

Directions: The above introduction gives some background and states the thesis. Rewrite it using each of the following introductory techniques, and try to include other style techniques you have learned.

2.　　Answer or ask a question.

Do you have trouble saying no to people? Of course it is hard to tell people you can't help them, to see their disappointed faces, and to feel that you've let them down. However, as you master saying no with grace, your disappointment will be eased. Remember, sometimes saying no honors the Lord because He has given us a limited number of hours each day to fill wisely. (Brianna Swanson)

3.　　Show the benefit gained.

There are so many benefits to saying no, including more time in your day. In many cases it can help you do what is right, and sometimes it can keep you out of trouble. (Bruce Cork)

4.　　End with an unexpected or humorous statement.

Would you be happy if your family was so busy that they found absolutely no time to spend with you? That's how Jesus feels when we're too busy to spend time with Him. So, please just say "no," and He'll thank you for it. (Samara Meahan)

5.   End with a suggested course of action.

Our saying no to too many activities honors the Lord. It's hard, but we must remember that the Lord gives help to those who ask. Just ask Him and He'll help. It's easy to fill up the day with so many activities that spark our interest. However, we must remember to guard out time and remember that sometimes saying no honors the Lord. Look to fellow believers of Christ for help in this difficult situation. (Amber Myers)

6.   End with a quotation or a familiar saying.

As Ecclesiastes 5:5 says, "It is better that you should not vow than that you should vow and not pay" (NASV). In other words, it's better not to promise to do something than to promise and not be able to do it. Next time, just say no—graciously. (Samara Meahan)

7.   Finish the story.

What happened to the lady crying on her couch? She finished her cry, got up and did her best at the tasks she had before her. But next time, she was careful to not bite off more than she could swallow. (Samara Meahan)

Chapter 7 Form Review Model—Editing Notes

Consequently,

Sometimes it takes years of teaching before we learn to wait. ^ ~~I~~t is much easier to forge ahead than

to stand still. There are hours of perplexity when the most willing spirit, anxiously desirous to serve the

Will it

Lord, does not know what path to take. Then what will it do? ^ ~~F~~ly back in cowardice, turn to the right

hand in fear, or rush forward in presumption? No, it must simply wait. <u>Wait in prayer, however</u>.

your   **You can**

Call on God and spread <u>the</u> case before Him. ^ ~~T~~ell Him your difficulty and plead His promise of

aid. In dilemmas between one duty and another, it is sweet to be humble as a child and wait with sim-

plicity of soul on the Lord. It is sure to be well with us when we are ~~heavily~~ willing to be guided by the

will of God. <u>But wait in faith</u>.

Faith expresses   **rather than**   **which**   **Him**

^ ~~Express~~ your unstaggering confidence in Him ^ unfaithful, untrusting waiting, ^ is an insult to ^

Believe that   **(Move to end of**

~~the~~ Lord. Believe that He will come at the right time. ^ ~~T~~he vision will come and will not tarry. [Wait in

paragraph) Do   **those troubles**

quiet patience,] ^ not ~~rebelling~~ because you are under the affliction, but ~~blessing~~ your God for ~~it~~. Never

murmur as the children of Israel did against Moses. Never wish you could go back to the world again,

but accept the case as it is and put it, without any self-will, into the hand of your covenant God~~,~~ saying,

(Save for conclusion)

"Now, Lord, not my will, but Yours be done. I do not know what to do. But I will wait until You

drive back my foes. I will wait, for my heart is fixed on You alone, O God, and my spirit waits for You

in the full conviction that You will be my joy and my salvation, my refuge and my strong tower."

Chapter 7—Form Review Model

Just Wait

In our modern culture, we hate to wait. We want everything now. With faster Internet connections and cellular phones, we can get immediate access to information and friends. We become frustrated if we have to wait even for a minute. It comes as a surprise and even a shock when the psalmist instructs us to "wait on the Lord" (Psalm 27:14).

Sometimes it takes years of teaching before we learn to wait. Consequently, it is much easier to forge ahead than to stand still. There are hours of perplexity when the most willing spirit, anxiously desirous to serve the Lord, does not know what path to take. Then what will it do? Will it fly back in cowardice, turn to the right hand in fear, or rush forward in presumption? No, it must simply wait. However, wait in prayer.

In prayer you may call on God and spread your case before Him. You can tell Him your difficulty and plead His promise of aid. In dilemmas between one duty and another, it is sweet to be humble as a child and wait with simplicity of soul on the Lord. When we are willing to be guided by the will of God, it is sure to be well with us. But wait in faith.

Faith expresses your unstaggering confidence in Him rather than unfaithful, untrusting waiting, which is an insult to the Lord. Believe that He will come at the right time. Believe that the vision will come and will not tarry. Do not rebel because you are under affliction, but bless your God for those troubles. Never murmur as the children of Israel did against Moses. Never wish you could go back to the world again, but accept the case as it is and put it, without any self-will, into the hand of your covenant God. Wait in quiet patience.

Although our society lacks patience and wants instant gratification, the Lord has bigger plans. He wants us to trust him. He wants us to say, "Now, Lord, not my will, but Yours be done. I do not know what to do. But I will wait until You drive back my foes. I will wait, for my heart is fixed on You alone, O God, and my spirit waits for You in the full conviction that You will be my joy and my salvation, my refuge and my strong tower." The Lord wants us to just wait.

Chapter 8—Thesis Models

1. **TV shows are always terrible.**
   Two problems: Contains a superlative (always) and a state of being verb. Additionally, it is not specific enough: Terrible how? Terrible why?

   <u>Better</u>: Too many TV shows encourage immorality.

2. **There were inconsistencies in the story line because the writers were on strike.**
   State of being verb (were), confusing position (What story line? What writers?), and a fact rather than an argument.

   <u>Better</u>: During the recent writers' strike, story line creativity suffered.

3. **Entertainment is a mind-numbing drug that people use to run away from the world.**
   Not bad. Has some interesting ideas. Tepid verbs though.

   <u>Better</u>: Acting as a mind-numbing drug, entertainment encourages people to abandon their responsibilities.

4. **There were many kinds of programs on the Discovery Channel.**
   State of being verb (were), lacks specificity, confusing position and focus (so what? How does this information apply to the topic? In fact, what is the topic?)

   <u>Better</u>: With the exception of programs on the Discovery Channel, television embraces a wearisome wasteland.

5. **TV is bad, bold, brazen, and boring.**
   State of being verb, wimpy word (bad), maybe a little too much alliteration.

   <u>Better</u>: Viewers need to protest brazen and boring shows.

6. **Movies are usually violent because so many murders and car crashes happen in them.**
   State of being verb (are), wimpy verb (happen), too specific (the number of murders and crashes would work well for evidence).
   <u>Better</u>: Television promotes violence because so many viewers mimic what they see on the tube.

7. **TV shows would be better if producers focused on three things: using less violence, showing less flesh, and to make their writers work harder.**
   Good ideas. Would be better if the "be" verb were replaced. Sentence also lacks parallelism (using, showing, to make). "Things" is one of those words that should be banned. It almost always can be replaced with something more specific.

   <u>Better</u>: To improve TV shows, producers need to focus on three areas: including less violence, showing less flesh, and making writers work harder.

8. **In our society, everyone blames entertainment for destroying the morals and minds of youth, but in actuality, entertainment is merely a scapegoat for others' failures.**
    I like this one. It offers an unusual perspective and piques my interest. I want to read more, which what a good thesis statement should do. It's not perfect, and I would like to see the "our" and "is" changed, but these difficulties are overshadowed by the unique thoughts.

    <u>Better</u>: In American society, everyone blames entertainment for destroying the morals and minds of youth, but in actuality, entertainment merely acts as a scapegoat for others' failures.

9. **By touting equality, television builds unity and understanding within communities.**
    Fine as is.

10. **Television promotes communication and compassion by exposing society to a variety of common situations.**
    Fine as is.

11. **When viewed with discernment, television programs create a smaller and more cohesive world by encouraging people to care and share.**
    Fine as is.

Chapter 8—Graphic Organizer Models
for Optional Exercises

Model #1

Most kids look for a scary monster like Frankenstein or the boogeyman underneath their parents' bed. When I look, I see a humongous collection of cow, kangaroo, alligator, lizard, and even ostrich leather boots all stuffed under my dad's side of the bed. This unique collection happens to belong to my accumulating dad. In addition to his boots, I admire my dad for his honorable character, his culinary skills, and unusual menageries.

My dad's protective character shone when my family drove to Berkeley, and a man unexpectedly punched him. After we got out of the car, we proceeded up the street, searching for the Extreme Pizza restaurant. As we were searching, we became confused because the advertised address for Extreme Pizza was actually a Jamba Juice. Standing there, perplexed, we heard, "Don't tell me about the moon!" Hearing this, my father turned around, and immediately, a man slugged my dad in the left eye. The gash bled profusely. The deranged man darted into a nearby book store. Seconds later, two strong, young black men pursued, tackled, and held the man down until the security guard and policeman arrived. Later, we found that the man was bi-polar. I was so proud of my dad for holding his temper and not retaliating. The man couldn't help being ill, and if my dad had punched him back, he could have become more violent and possibly harmed all of us. By displaying fortitude, my dad protected his family.

Model #2

Not only will a single-payer healthcare system hurt the economy, but it will also cut the quality of medical treatment. With government paying for healthcare, it will also control what doctors do so that it can save money. This strategy proved to be almost fatal to twenty-eight year-old Melissa Matthews, who lives in the UK, which suffers from universal healthcare. She suspected that she had bowel cancer and had gone through many tests. The doctor said there was nothing to worry about and sent her home. A week later, the cancer reached a critical stage, and Matthews was rushed to the A and E. There, doctors discovered a large tumor in her bowel and were forced to remove her womb and some of her colon. It turns out that the doctor based his diagnosis on government statistics. Statistically, Matthews was too young to have bowel cancer. Statistically, there was a low chance of her having bowel cancer so the doctor did not bother to do more tests when the first test turned out inconclusive (Donnelly). Basing diagnosis and treatment of a patient on statistics endangers his or her safety. Not every patient is the same. However, doctors in the UK can do little about situations like this since they have to follow government procedures.

Donnelly, Laura. "Patients with Suspected Cancer Forced to Wait So NHS Targets Can Be Hit." *The Daily Telegraph* [London] 7 June 2009, n. pag. Web. 6 July 2010.

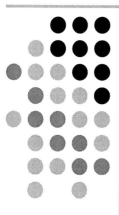

APPENDIX B

Grading Sheets

How do you know if you are doing well on the elegant essay exercises?

Checklists and reminders follow.

Name: _____   Date: _____

Class: _____   Score Sheet

Course Score Sheet for Checklist Method

Assignment	Date Turned In	Score	Possible	Comments
Exercises				
Exercise 2			40	
Exercise 4a			50	
Exercise 4b			40	
Exercise 6			40	
Exercise 8			40	
Exercise 11			40	
Exercise 13			50	
Exercise 15			20	
Essays				
Desc. Draft			95	
Desc. Final			100	
Pers. Draft			95	
Pers. Final			100	
Quizzes				
Quiz #1			10	
Quiz #2			10	
Quiz #3			10	
Quiz #4			10	
Quiz #5			10	
Quiz #6			10	
Total				
			770	

A range: 693 - 770; B range: 616 - 692; C range: 539 - 615; D range: 462 - 538

Thesis Statement Grading Sheet

Exercise 2

Steps to create a thesis statement

1. Determine your essay's intent. Will it inform, describe, or persuade?
2. Narrow your focus or your topic.
3. Develop a two-part statement. In part one, state your narrow focus. In part two, add details concerning what you want to say about it.

Checklist

☐ Make sure your thesis statements do not cover too much ground. Your thesis should summarize or preview your essay, not duplicate it.

☐ Make sure academic thesis statements are parallel.

☐ Remember, thesis statements may be only one sentence for these exercises.

☐ Check that your persuasive thesis statement presents an argument rather than state a fact.

☐ Check that your narrative thesis statement creates an emotion or alludes to a lesson learned.

Structure

Descriptive or narrative thesis   _____ 10

Informative or expository thesis   _____ 10

Persuasive or argumentative thesis   _____ 10

Academic three-pronged academic thesis (marked as such)   _____ 10

Total _____ 40

Optional Pop Quiz   _____ 10

Support & Evidence Grading Sheet

Exercises 4a & 4b

Checklist

☐ Is your paragraph understandable? Good topic, clincher, and flow?

☐ Does your evidence support the assertion?

☐ Over the course of the two exercises (4a & 4b), do you use four *different* kinds of support?

☐ Do you *show* rather than *tell*?

☐ What is done well? What might be improved?

Structure

Ex. 4a Paragraph One   _____ 10

Ex. 4a Paragraph Two   _____ 10

Ex. 4b Paragraph Three   _____ 10

Ex. 4b Paragraph Four   _____ 10

Style

Paragraphs exhibit good syntax (variety of sentence openers and construction), diction (word choices), and flair (dress-ups and decorations).

_____ 5

Mechanics

Fewer than 3 grammar/spelling/punctuation errors on each exercise

(If fewer than 3 errors, give the full 5 points. Deduct 1 point for each error over 3. If more than 8 errors, give the student a zero.)

_____ 5

Total _____ 50

Optional Pop Quiz   _____ 10

Transitions Grading Sheet

Exercise 6

Checklist

- ☐ Did you include yellow line (reference) and road sign (connective) transitions to tie each sentence to the previous one?
- ☐ Do your transitions make sense? Do they keep the reader on track?
- ☐ Do you use a variety of transitional techniques rather than over-rely on one?
- ☐ Do you use a *Synonym Finder* or thesaurus to look up synonyms? Does the vocabulary work in context?
- ☐ When illustrating a point with a Bible verse (or other quotation), do you transition to it? You might include a phrase such as "As [Bible verse] illustrates…" or "In [Bible verse] God says…" Watch for this, especially in the Spurgeon excerpts.
- ☐ Do you punctuate Bible verses correctly?
  <u>Correct</u>: He said, "Excuse me." <u>Incorrect</u>: He said, "Excuse me".
  <u>Correct</u> Bible verse citation: "Jesus wept" (John 11:35). <u>Note</u> no period after *wept*. It goes after the right parenthesis.
- ☐ Do you combine sentences in the exercises where needed?

Structure

Variety of yellow line transitions   _____ 20

Variety of road sign transitions   _____ 20

Total _____ 40

Optional Pop Quiz   _____ 10

Introductions Grading Sheet

Exercise 8

Checklist

☐ Rewrite the entire introductory paragraph in the exercises rather than just tacking on another sentence, such as a question, startling statement, or quotation.

☐ Feel free to add style and change some of the words, especially the verbs.

☐ When adding creative details, be careful to not stray too far away from the original topic.

☐ Be sure dialogue or a startling statement connects with the rest of the introduction.

☐ Banned statements: Anything similar to "By reading this essay…" or "I intend to show…" or "By way of introduction. . . ."

☐ No "I" statements in the introduction: "I think," "I believe," others. <u>Exception</u>: If you are relating personal experience, "I" statements are fine.

☐ Make sure the introduction makes sense and uses appropriate transitions.

Structure

Question   _____ 5

Benefit   _____ 5

Startling or humorous statement   _____ 5

Quotation or famous saying   _____ 5

Dialogue   _____ 5

Description   _____ 5

Style

Introductions exhibit varied syntax (variety of sentence openers and construction), diction (word choices), and flair (dress-ups and decorations).

                                                     _____ 5

Mechanics

Fewer than 3 grammar/spelling/punctuation errors on exercise.

(If fewer than 3 errors, give the full 5 points. Deduct 1 point for each error over 3. If more than 8 errors, give the student a zero.)

                                                     _____ 5

                                              Total _____ 40

Optional Pop Quiz   _____ 10

Conclusions Grading Sheet

Exercise 11

Checklist

☐ Refrain from introducing any new information. If you want to discuss a new topic, add another body paragraph.

☐ Make an application or suggest a course of action based on information you have already discussed.

☐ Emphasize the most important point or what you want the reader to remember.

☐ Tie up any loose ends and reward your reader for reading.

☐ Never, ever begin with "In conclusion."

☐ No "I" statements. (Exception: personal experience)

☐ Write the entire conclusion rather than just the concluding technique.

☐ Make sure the conclusion makes sense and uses appropriate transitions.

Structure

Question   _____ 5

Benefit   _____ 5

Startling or humorous statement   _____ 5

Quotation or famous saying   _____ 5

Suggested course of action   _____ 5

Finish the story   _____ 5

Style

Conclusions exhibit varied syntax (variety of sentence openers and construction), diction (word choices), and flair (dress-ups and decorations).

                                                      _____ 5

Mechanics

Fewer than 3 grammar/spelling/punctuation errors on exercise.

(If fewer than 3 errors, give the full 5 points. Deduct 1 point for each error over 3. If more than 8 errors, give the student a zero.)

                                                      _____ 5

                                        Total _____ 40

Optional Pop Quiz   _____ 10

Form Review Grading Sheet

Exercise 13

Checklist

☐ Try changing some of Spurgeon's archaic words or rearranging his sentences.

☐ Correct Bible verse punctuation: "The Bible verse" (I Address 11:14). Note that the period occurs after the right parenthesis, not inside the Bible verse's quotation mark.

☐ If you are shaky on a particular concept (thesis, transitions, introductions, or conclusions), be sure to review that section in your book.

☐ Pay particular attention to bridge transitions or paragraph hooks.

Structure

Thesis   _____ 10

Transitions   _____ 10

Introduction   _____ 10

Conclusion   _____ 10

Style

Essays exhibit varied syntax (variety of sentence openers and construction), diction (word choices), and flair (dress-ups and decorations).

                                           _____ 5

Mechanics

Fewer than 3 grammar/spelling/punctuation errors on exercise.

(If fewer than 3 errors, give the full 5 points. Deduct 1 point for each error over 3. If more than 8 errors, give the student a zero.)

                                           _____ 5

                                  Total _____ 50

Thesis & Outline Grading Sheet

Exercise 15

Checklist

When evaluating or creating thesis statements, keep these criteria in mind.

☐ Banned: universals, superlatives, hyperbole

☐ Banned: state-of-being or linking verbs (is, am, are, was, were, be, being, been)

☐ Check for parallelism.

☐ Where appropriate, use clausal words: *when, while, where, as, since, if,* or *although* (www.asia)

☐ For persuasive essays, does the thesis make a claim or argument?

☐ Is the topic specific and narrow? Does it need to be qualified?

☐ Include zip: active verbs, strong word choices, and careful alliteration

☐ Ask these four questions: Does the thesis answer the prompt? Does it take a specific position? Does it pass the *how* or *why* test? Does it provide enough focus?

Structure

Your teacher will choose the best ten thesis statements to evaluate. Each is worth two points: one point for the evaluation and one point for your reasoning/improvement.

1. _____ 2   4. _____ 2   7. _____ 2   9. _____ 2

2. _____ 2   5. _____ 2   8. _____ 2   10. _____ 2

3. _____ 2   6. _____ 2

Total _____ 20

Optional Pop Quiz   _____ 10

Descriptive Essay Grading Sheet (Draft)

Introduction _____ / 10 points
- Captures reader's attention
- Establishes the significance of the topic
- Contains a well-formulated thesis

_____

_____

Body Paragraphs _____ / 60 points total (20 for each paragraph)
Circle excellent, good, fair, or poor, and then check the boxes to indicate a problem area.

Body Paragraph I	Body Paragraph II	Body Paragraph III
Excellent, Good, Fair, Poor	Excellent, Good, Fair, Poor	Excellent, Good, Fair, Poor
☐ Topic/thesis connect?	☐ Topic/thesis connect?	☐ Topic/thesis connect?
☐ Stays on topic?	☐ Stays on topic?	☐ Stays on topic?
☐ Clear explanation?	☐ Clear explanation?	☐ Clear explanation?
☐ Clincher statement?	☐ Clincher statement?	☐ Clincher statement?
☐ Descriptive imagery?	☐ Descriptive imagery?	☐ Descriptive imagery?
Support:	Support:	Support:
☐ example, personal experience, statistics, research, observation, description, anecdote/story, analogy	☐ example, personal experience, statistics, research, observation, description, anecdote/story, analogy	☐ example, personal experience, statistics, research, observation, description, anecdote/story, analogy

Conclusion _____ / 10 points
- Revisits thesis
- Leaves reader with something to think about
- Leaves a feeling of completeness

_____

_____

Grammar & Style _____ / 15 points
- Varied syntax, diction, and creativity
- Correctly formatted citations & Works Cited Page
- Fewer than 3 spelling/punctuation errors overall

Total _____ 95

Comments:

Descriptive Essay Grading Sheet (Final)

Introduction _____ / 10 points

    Captures reader's attention

    Establishes the significance of the topic

    Contains a well-formulated thesis

_____

_____

Body Paragraphs _____ / 60 points total (20 for each paragraph)

Circle excellent, good, fair, or poor, and then check the boxes to indicate a problem area.

Body Paragraph I	Body Paragraph II	Body Paragraph III
Excellent, Good, Fair, Poor	Excellent, Good, Fair, Poor	Excellent, Good, Fair, Poor
☐ Topic/thesis connect?	☐ Topic/thesis connect?	☐ Topic/thesis connect?
☐ Stays on topic?	☐ Stays on topic?	☐ Stays on topic?
☐ Clear explanation?	☐ Clear explanation?	☐ Clear explanation?
☐ Clincher statement?	☐ Clincher statement?	☐ Clincher statement?
☐ Descriptive imagery?	☐ Descriptive imagery?	☐ Descriptive imagery?
Support:	Support:	Support:
☐ example, personal experience, statistics, research, observation, description, anecdote/story, analogy	☐ example, personal experience, statistics, research, observation, description, anecdote/story, analogy	☐ example, personal experience, statistics, research, observation, description, anecdote/story, analogy

Conclusion _____ / 10 points

    Revisits thesis

    Leaves reader with something to think about

    Leaves a feeling of completeness

_____

_____

Grammar & Style _____ / 20 points

    Varied syntax, diction, and creativity

    Correctly formatted citations and Works Cited Page

    Fewer than 3 spelling/punctuation errors overall

Total _____ 100

Comments:

Name: _____   Date: _____

Class: _____   Chapter 10

Persuasive Essay Grading Sheet (Draft)

Introduction _____ / 10 points
    Captures reader's attention
    Establishes the significance of the topic
    Contains a well-formulated thesis

_____
_____

Body Paragraphs _____ / 60 points total (20 for each paragraph)
Circle excellent, good, fair, or poor, and then check the boxes to indicate a problem area.

Body Paragraph I	Body Paragraph II	Body Paragraph III
Excellent, Good, Fair, Poor	Excellent, Good, Fair, Poor	Excellent, Good, Fair, Poor
☐ Topic/thesis connect?	☐ Topic/thesis connect?	☐ Topic/thesis connect?
☐ Stays on topic?	☐ Stays on topic?	☐ Stays on topic?
☐ Clear explanation?	☐ Clear explanation?	☐ Clear explanation?
☐ Clincher statement?	☐ Clincher statement?	☐ Clincher statement?
☐ Persuasive argument?	☐ Persuasive argument?	☐ Persuasive argument?
Support:	Support:	Support:
☐ example, personal experience, statistics, research, observation, description, anecdote/story, analogy	☐ example, personal experience, statistics, research, observation, description, anecdote/story, analogy	☐ example, personal experience, statistics, research, observation, description, anecdote/story, analogy

Conclusion _____ / 10 points
    Revisits thesis
    Leaves reader with something to think about
    Leaves a feeling of completeness

_____
_____

Grammar & Style _____ / 15 points
    Varied syntax, diction, and creativity
    Correctly formatted citations and Works Cited Page
    Fewer than 3 spelling/punctuation errors overall

                                                   Total _____ 95

Comments:

Persuasive Essay Grading Sheet (Final)

Introduction _____ / 10 points
> Captures reader's attention
> Establishes the significance of the topic
> Contains a well-formulated thesis

_____

_____

Body Paragraphs _____ / 60 points total (20 for each paragraph)
Circle excellent, good, fair, or poor, and then check the boxes to indicate a problem area.

Body Paragraph I	Body Paragraph II	Body Paragraph III
Excellent, Good, Fair, Poor	Excellent, Good, Fair, Poor	Excellent, Good, Fair, Poor
☐ Topic/thesis connect?	☐ Topic/thesis connect?	☐ Topic/thesis connect?
☐ Stays on topic?	☐ Stays on topic?	☐ Stays on topic?
☐ Clear explanation?	☐ Clear explanation?	☐ Clear explanation?
☐ Clincher statement?	☐ Clincher statement?	☐ Clincher statement?
☐ Persuasive argument?	☐ Persuasive argument?	☐ Persuasive argument?
Support:	Support:	Support:
☐ example, personal experience, statistics, research, observation, description, anecdote/story, analogy	☐ example, personal experience, statistics, research, observation, description, anecdote/story, analogy	☐ example, personal experience, statistics, research, observation, description, anecdote/story, analogy

Conclusion _____ / 10 points
> Revisits thesis
> Leaves reader with something to think about
> Leaves a feeling of completeness

_____

_____

Grammar & Style _____ / 20 points
> Varied syntax, diction, and creativity
> Correctly formatted citations and Works Cited Page
> Fewer than 3 spelling/punctuation errors overall

Total _____ 100

Comments:

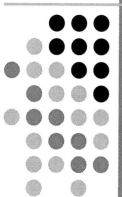

APPENDIX C

IEW Essay Model & Style Techniques

Basic Essay Model & Style Review

The Elegant Essay is about structure (form or organization) and content (ideas). To profitably use it, students do not have to have any background in the other three essay areas such as style (syntax/sentences, diction/words), mechanics (grammar) or voice (personality or overall expression).

On the other hand, many of you already have some background, and you don't want to lose it.

If you have taken previous structure and style lessons from the Institute for Excellence in Writing (IEW), you may want to review the basic essay model and the style guides before beginning *The Elegant Essay* lessons. Additionally, you should keep practicing what you have learned as you do the exercises and write the essays asked for in this book. You know the old saying: Use it or lose it.

The Game Is Over

This is very important: You *do not* need to include all of the style techniques in every paragraph you write as you did when you were learning them. For example, you do need to use a variety of sentence openers. You do not need to use one of each of the techniques in every paragraph. You should use the style techniques you've learned when they fit your purpose. Otherwise, your writing will sound formulaic. If you have previously included something like all six sentence openers, two dress-ups, and one decoration in each paragraph, it's time to rethink your style and use only what will benefit your essay.

How do you know what will benefit your essay? Use your inner ear. Read your essay aloud to see if it "sounds right." Basically what you want to do is develop your writing voice and infuse your essay with your unique personality. Your writing should sound passionate and powerful, not stilted and stiff. It should sound like a conversation—depending on your audience, a formal one with a professor, an informal one with a peer, or a colloquial one with a friend. Use the style techniques that will help you achieve your purpose.

IEW Style Reminders

Dress-Ups—use as necessary

1. *who-which* clause
2. "-ly"
3. *because* clause
4. strong verb
5. quality adjective
6. *when, while, where, as, since, if although* clause

(Advanced: dual adverbs, verbs, adjectives; noun clause; adverbial or adjectival "teeter-totters")

Sentence Openers—use often

1. subject
2. preposition
3. "-ly" word
4. -ing,
5. clausal (www.asia.bu)
6. VVS (very short sentence)
7. advanced: "-ed"

Decorations—use sparingly

1. question
2. conversation
3. 3sss
4. dramatic opening/closing
5. simile or metaphor
6. alliteration

Triple Extensions (Advanced)—use sparingly

1. word repetition
2. phrase & clausal repetition
3. repeating "-ings," consecutive or spaced
4. repeating "-lys," consecutive or spaced
5. repeating adjectives or nouns
6. repeating verbs, consecutive or spaced

"-ly" Adverb List

abruptly
absently
absentmindedly
accusingly
actually
adversely
affectionately
amazingly
angrily
anxiously
arrogantly
bashfully
beautifully
boldly
bravely
breathlessly
brightly
briskly
broadly
calmly
carefully
carelessly
certainly
cheaply
cheerfully
cleanly
clearly
cleverly
closely
clumsily
coaxingly
commonly
compassionate-ly
conspicuously
continually
coolly
correctly
crisply
crossly
curiously
daintily
dangerously

darkly
dearly
deceivingly
delicately
delightfully
desperately
determinedly
diligently
disgustingly
distinctly
doggedly
dreamily
emptily
energetically
enormously
enticingly
entirely
enviously
especially
evenly
exactly
excitedly
exclusively
expertly
extremely
fairly
faithfully
famously
fearlessly
ferociously
fervently
finally
foolishly
fortunately
frankly
frantically
freely
frenetically
frightfully
fully
furiously
generally
generously

gently
gleefully
gratefully
greatly
greedily
grumpily
guiltily
happily
harshly
hatefully
heartily
heavily
helpfully
helplessly
highly
hopelessly
hungrily
immediately
importantly
impulsively
inadvertently
increasingly
incredibly
innocently
instantly
intensely
intently
inwardly
jokingly
kindly
knowingly
lawfully
lightly
likely
longingly
loudly
madly
marvelously
meaningfully
mechanically
meekly
mentally
messily

mindfully
miserably
mockingly
mostly
mysteriously
naturally
nearly
neatly
negatively
nervously
nicely
obviously
occasionally
oddly
openly
outwardly
partially
passionately
patiently
perfectly
perpetually
playfully
pleasantly
pleasingly
politely
poorly
positively
potentially
powerfully
professionally
properly
proudly
quaveringly
queerly
quickly
quietly
quintessentially
rapidly
rapturously
ravenously
readily
reassuringly
regretfully

reluctantly
reproachfully
restfully
righteously
rightfully
rigidly
rudely
sadly
safely
scarcely
searchingly
sedately
seemingly
selfishly
separately
seriously
sharply
sheepishly
sleepily
slowly
slyly
softly
solidly
speedily
sternly
stingily
strictly
stubbornly
successfully
superstitiously
surprisingly
suspiciously
sympathetically
tenderly
terribly
thankfully
thoroughly
thoughtfully
tightly
totally
tremendously
triumphantly
truly

truthfully
understandably
unfairly
unfortunately
unhappily
unwillingly
urgently
usually
utterly
vastly
venomously
viciously
violently
warmly
wearily
wholly
wildly
willfully
wisely
wonderfully
wonderingly
worriedly

-ly imposters

chilly
friendly
ghastly
ghostly
holy
kingly
knightly
lonely
lovely
orderly
prickly
queenly
surly
ugly
worldly
wrinkly

Preposition List

aboard
about
above
according to
across
after
against
along
amid
among
around
aside
at
because of
before
behind
below
beneath
beside
between

beyond
by
concerning
despite
down
during
except
for
from
in
inside
instead of
into
like
minus
near
of
off
on
opposite

out
outside
over
past
since
through
throughout
to
toward
under
underneath
unlike
until
up
upon
with
within
without